Empath

and

Narcissist

A Guide to Heal Childhood Trauma With Effective Exercises

(Hundle Narcissists and Finally Stop the Emotional Storm Coming From Others and Yourself)

Thomas Kaufman

Published By **Andrew Zen**

Thomas Kaufman

Empath and Narcissist: A Guide to Heal Childhood Trauma With Effective Exercises (Handle Narcissists and Finally Stop the Emotional Storm Coming From Others and Yourself)

ISBN   978-1-990373-74-9

No part of this guidebook shall be reproduced in any form without permission in writing from the publisher except in the case of brief quotations embodied in critical articles or reviews.

Legal & Disclaimer

The information contained in this book is not designed to replace or take the place of any form of medicine or professional medical advice. The information in this book has been provided for educational & entertainment purposes only.

The information contained in this book has been compiled from sources deemed reliable, and it is accurate to the best of the Author's knowledge; however, the Author cannot guarantee its accuracy and validity and cannot be held liable for any errors or omissions. Changes are periodically made to this book. You must consult your doctor or get professional medical advice before using any of the suggested remedies, techniques, or information in this book.

Table Of Contents

Chapter 1: What Is An Empath?

00003.Jpeg

An Empath is said to be someone who has a magical capability to virtually "step into" america of a of some other individual. Empaths are as a substitute sensitive beings who can surely revel in and feel the feelings and feelings of various human beings. If an individual is an Empath, they may enjoy deep emotions past what someone else is actively expressing. This manner that regardless of the reality that an character is alternatively gifted at hiding their feelings or protecting them with one-of-a-kind feelings, an Empath can sense, enjoy, and intricately apprehend the proper feelings of that person. Not best can the Empath revel in and experience those feelings, however they also can apprehend them on a deep stage.

Empaths have the ability to experience entire empathy in the direction of truely anybody and all people else. They can experience it in the direction of circle of relatives, pals, buddies, youngsters, strangers, animals, flora, and even inanimate items. Some humans are recognized to be more empathetic within the course of nice subjects over others. This is regularly how we come to be with such things as "animal whisperers" or "plant whisperers." When this takes location, that precise individual is thought to be greater empathetic closer to that which they may supposedly "whisper" to. What is truly happening is not a whisper, however as an opportunity a deep inner knowing of what the possibility's wishes are.

If someone is an Empath, they're no longer restrained through time and region. In truth, they're not in reality restricted at all. An Empath can experience the feelings and intellectual state of oldsters which can be extensively far away. Some may even sense the feelings and intellectual u.S. Of the usa of human beings who've lengthy thinking about passed. For example, if they had been to visit a museum and notice the assets of someone who existed a few years within the beyond but whom has due to the truth passed away, a few Empaths can step without delay into the feelings and energies of that individual. This lets in Empaths to be deeply information and to have a rather particular mind-set of the vicinity round them. Where does empathic energy come from?

The query of wherein empathic powers come from, or how humans come to personal them, is one that generation though does not have a strong solution. But there are some theories. There is clearly loads of proof to indicate that a "normal" diploma of empathy is to be had to most humans in early improvement. Newborn toddlers in neonatal gadgets display an lack of capacity to differentiate private feelings from the ones around them; if one toddler starts offevolved to cry, usually maximum others will observe in form right away, as they're no longer but conscious that this ache or anxiety isn't theirs to private. Most toddlers who gather a wholesome amount of care and hobby will keep mimicry and emotional enmeshment sooner or later of the primary few years of life--that is how children can study speech and motion. Some children, raised in specifically tight-knit households or organizations, may also war on the start to apprehend the feature of pronouns that distinguish between the person self and the organization, posing questions like, "Mama, why are we unhappy in recent times?" when they have a look at this emotion in any other man or woman.

Those who endure in thoughts inside the supernatural possibilities of empathic electricity moreover have a tendency to suppose that satisfactory humans are fated to acquire these offers and that empaths revel in as they do to serve a few better motive as decided via cosmic or holy format. This notion regularly coincides with the belief that empaths are born specific, and not shaped via the use of using their surroundings; even as the volume of energy they personal or how they channel energy may additionally vary for the duration of their lives, their heightened sensitivity is taken into consideration an innate trait.

Conversely, there are folks that accept as true with empathic abilities come from the environment or sports wherein a person is raised, as a feature of nurture instead of nature. Many psychologists take a look at that children raised in volatile, neglectful, or volatile households research early immediately to come across subtle adjustments of their mother and father' behaviors as a crucial coping capacity and safety mechanism, allowing them to are looking ahead to, avoid, or perhaps save you traumatic episodes.

Parents might not always be evil or malicious in raising a infant who develops excessive empathic sensitivity. Some theories posit that the best environmental element had to cause any such improvement is an older authoritative parent inside the little one's life which calls for the kid to empathize with them frequently. For example, a decide who is grieving the loss of a cherished one might probably, with out ever proceeding to, compel their toddler to empathize with a diploma of emotional pain which they haven't but been prepared for, and can not often even realize at the sort of younger age. A child who's located on this characteristic often enough may moreover never analyze to differentiate their very personal feelings from those of others, and can even struggle to experience that they will be actual, big, or whole with out the have an impact on of a few extraordinary dominant character. They turn out to be hyper-focused on being concerned for the parental determine of their existence, and in no way learn how to acquire care with out guilt, disgrace or tension, as maximum kids do.

Once a toddler develops this capability, it's miles exceptional natural for them to keep the use of it outside the residence, amongst friends, colleagues, fans, or maybe strangers. There also are folks who be aware this identical abilities of allergic reaction rising for the first time in entire-grown adults while they're romantically concerned (or otherwise firmly bonded) with an abusive character kind, along with a narcissist.

It is in truth nicely well worth noting that many empaths first grow to be aware of their heightened sensitivity inside the course of relationships with parents that are empathy horrible. Furthermore, whether or not or not they'll be aware of their capabilities or now not, empaths are so frequently worried with narcissists, sociopaths and psychopaths, that many wonders if empathic energy skills as a form of invisible beacon to the ones who have those character disorders. The concept that empaths and empathy poor types are inquisitive about every exclusive like magnets begs the question-which generally comes first? The empathic power or the abusive surroundings wherein it turns into a important information for survival? While it makes feel that empathic talents expand as a response to abuse and trauma, it's also absolutely viable that abuse and trauma might possibly always exist in any case, and empaths are surely drawn to these environments more than maximum humans. An unlucky truth of existence for the empath who has not however clearly awakened to their electricity is that they'll frequently experience compassion for those whom every person else has deserted, failing to see that those souls have been left on my own for a terrific reason and aren't worth of the empath's care or hobby. It have to mean that abusive times and relationships are like traps which empaths are specifically vulnerable to falling into, as opposed to the cause or catalyst for heightened sensitivity.

Thus a long way, technology has no longer been capable of provide evidence one way or the alternative, however some present day findings might also permit for each possibilities to coexist. The take a look at of epigenetics issues how our genetic cloth is impacted through way of our research and environment, which means that that we skip on more to our youngsters through our DNA than honestly a blueprint for the frame. With the invention of epigenetics, we are now capable of theorize that trauma ought to have an intergenerational ripple impact, leaving a protracted-lasting mark at the descendants of patients, whether or not or no longer or now not those descendants are really privy to the trauma or no longer. That could allow a soul to be born with empathic abilties which might be right away innate and a developed response to abuse.

There are many viable property of empathic capability, and new records is continuously surfacing to growth our facts of it. Likewise, the medical region has but to firmly define the purpose of empathy-deficient character troubles, nor that of situations like autism and Asperger's syndrome. Some consider those emotional states or situations feed into every one of a kind, like two species sharing a symbiotic courting, or an actual embodiment of yin and yang energies. Others although accept as true with there are only biological reasons for situations that fall on every ends of the empathy scale. Then, of route, there are folks who see the empathy scale as a circle in region of a line, believing that someone with an overabundance of new empathic functionality can evolve right into a narcissist or vice versa.

Whatever you consider, one thing is obvious. Empathic capability need to be understood, professional, and balanced to be part of a wholesome, glad life-style.

Advantages of Being an Empath

Highly sensitive people may have a low opinion of themselves, but being an empath isn't always some component to be resented; there are numerous blessings to being one.

1. You can spot liars

We stay in a global in which truth is uncommon. There are liars anywhere. Thus, in case you aren't cautious, you can run into problem. But being an empath, you have the functionality to spot those who are telling lies. This capability shields you in opposition to their malicious purpose. Once you recognize that someone is telling lies you short apprehend what shape of individual they'll be. Considering the risky reactions that liars elicit, it is vital that an empath has a entire information of what's taking place. Having the ability to perceive liars approach that you can live out of hassle, but you have to additionally assist your close to contacts.

2. Healing

The fashion of ailments on this global is sudden. Some of them can be cured the use of mainstream strategies whilst others can not. Some empaths own the winning of delivering human beings from illnesses. Empaths who've the capacity to heal others play a pivotal position in society. They assist reduce human suffering this is due to disease dealers, and at the equal time, clinical empaths help us entice incredible human beings into our lives. One of the best joys of existence is having an army of reliable friends and own family who will manual your goals and desires. Being a medical empath also empowers you to restore damaged relationships.

three. Sharp Senses

The common character doesn't have nearly as effective senses. Empaths have a miles more advanced sense of fragrance, contact, sight, and listening to. Empaths can select out up on the slightest adjustments and nuances in a placing. For example, if you are hanging out in a corridor, and the temperatures bypass a notch excessive, an empath may also additionally apprehend the temperature change. Having sharp senses bolsters your reflexes, and this allows you to act pretty speedy. Having sharp listening abilties draws humans to you, and puts them in a submissive frame. Empaths employ their sharp senses to discover the arena, giving them new perspectives, and extra importantly, gaining idea.

4. Comfortable being on my own

Going for long stretches of time without human touch will truely invite boredom and loneliness into your existence. Most human beings will be predisposed to stay with their toxic companions because of the reality they might occasionally function on the identical time as they're on my own. But empaths virtually crave to be on my own. When they spend their day blending with different humans thru the save you of that day they'll be uninterested in physical strength. Thus for an empath, being on my own is not a reason for resentment, but sincerely a welcome deal with. Empaths want to be careful not to overdo something but to clearly strike a balance among spending time with others and maintaining apart themselves.

5. Creativity

Empaths own numerous creative power. They have a special manner of searching at human beings and situations. An empath will pour their modern electricity into every interest of theirs simply so they will stand out. Naturally, empaths have a propensity to select up careers as a manner to allow them to express their creative issue. Some of those careers encompass developing a tune, drawing, and modeling. Considering the quite sensitive nature of empaths, they want to start their careers within the modern international at an inordinately more youthful age, simply so they may growth a thick skin and come to be familiar with the hostilities of human beings.

6. Kind and respectful

We live in a worldwide wherein kindness is typically turning into unusual. In its location, we have jingoism and self-absorption. When you are type, you display the sector which you respect others. And humans are in particular right at sniffing the kind ones from the not-so-kind ones. Most human beings seem to anticipate that kind humans are weaklings, however they couldn't be greater misled. Actually, type humans keep masses of electricity, and this is demonstrated in their difficulty and generosity.

7. A awesome courting with animals

It's not unusual data that pets are a protracted way extra reliable than your buddies. Every home canine adores their proprietor, however if the owner is an empath, their relationship becomes even tighter. Having a real connection with your pets is an excellent element that empowers you to be the fine draw close. Recent research have validated that animals device feelings. This technique they register how numerous human beings address them. Empaths don't have some thing but love for our bushy pals. Some empaths can also even talk with animals at the telepathic stage.

eight. Being aware of one-of-a-kind human beings's emotions

A man or ladies is certainly a most complex being. Emotions play a massive position in the picks that we make. Good feelings cause correct actions, but horrible emotions result in horrible moves. The common individual cannot frequently inform an person's feelings from simply looking at them. But there are empaths who can perceive distinct people's power and emotions. It's a great functionality because it facilitates the empath weigh his terms efficiently. The empath seems to be typically prepared with genuinely the proper terms. When you start to apprehend one-of-a-kind human beings's emotions, you furthermore can also moreover begin paying attention to your emotions, and it allows you expand in a wholesome fashion.

nine. Predicting the destiny

People will continuously be intrigued with the useful resource of the destiny. Every individual in the world seems in advance to day after today, to the future, with the hopes of making their lifestyles better. Can absolutely everyone because it have to be predict what's going to appear? Many human beings have come out offering bizarre theories whose outcomes never noticed the light of day. But being an empath, you may have the present of looking into the destiny. Even even though you're an empath, you may though need the assist of different people, so you can also damage down the findings and do away with mistakes.

10. A great lover

Empaths make the tremendous fanatics. This is partially due to the fact they have got a immoderate emotional funding. An empath will usually pour out their coronary coronary heart in case you need to tighten their bond. The worst aspect that might seem to an empath is unreciprocated love. Empaths also are careful of those terrible trends that would threaten the stability in their courting.

11. Above-not unusual intelligence

This won't be the case for every empath available, however most of them percentage a familiar story of now not becoming in during their early life, after which turning to books, or one-of-a-kind activities so that you can distract themselves from their pain. Of direction, intelligence is the byproduct of a palms-on method to solving problems. Empaths moreover have a tendency to be deep thinkers who are worried approximately the future of our global, and the subjects in it.

12. Aware of beauty

Thanks to their "specific" manner of perceiving existence, empaths can see many stuff that stay ignorant of the not unusual eye. If you're an empath, you may have a addiction of noticing numerous splendor workplace work and figures and grow to be more appreciative of Mother Nature. Most empaths are happiest even as no individual is bothering them, while they're by myself and attractive within the sports activities that their soul dreams.

thirteen. Great pal

As an empath, you have had been given the recognition of being a sincerely tremendous man who will save you at now not anything to make his friends glad. Empaths are deeply emotional humans, and they love developing profound reminiscences in order to live etched in their minds. Empaths like taking off with their small circle of relied on buddies and function a blast. In as a excellent deal as empaths make exceptional buddies, they ought to protect themselves in opposition to abusive human beings. Empaths are magnets for human beings with abusive personalities, simply so they want to be cautious lest they go through.

14. Figuring out a person's in hassle

As an empath, you comprehend that commonly while you contemplate or dream that a person is going via a worry, it usually is the case. As an empath, it can be not unusual for you to call a person and the primary factor that comes out in their mouth is a confession that they're going through a hard patch, and have been, in reality, thinking about calling you before you honestly did. This functionality may moreover moreover sound creepy before everything. It isn't. Empaths are in order that emotionally superior than the common person. This is glaringly a completely unique capability, and empaths need to use it liberally.

15. Taking care of the environment

Human beings appear to have a unfavourable power that permeates almost all areas of life. When you look at something deserving of protection and appreciate, you may find out that it's miles lengthy defiled. For an empath, you've got got got the planet's hobby at heart. You are careful of defensive the environment and also you sensitize others on the significance of looking after each the planet and the surroundings.

16. You understand people

As an empath, you have got the unusual gift of looking someone and making an accurate judgment concerning their thoughts-set, person, and man or woman. This skills is essential in terms of comparing human beings's resourcefulness. When you recognize what a person is like, you will be inclined to address them with empathy, and it'll make your relationship more profitable.

Challenges of Being An Empath

Every coin has elements, and actually as being an empath has its powerful side, it additionally has traumatic situations.

Empaths enjoy deeply. Yes, a few difficulty may be both a blessing and a mission. Because empaths experience deeply, conditions can harm more and cause more pressure. At times, being an empath with out self-safety can harm your fitness or fitness.

Empaths are sensitive. Sometimes, it appears, too sensitive. This is associated with feeling deeply. Empaths generally have a tendency to internalize criticism, emotions, and conditions that other people may additionally push aside.

Empaths are magnets for humans with troubles and for power vampires. Empaths usually generally tend to draw people with issues. This reasons an emotional and bodily drain on empaths and can damage their fitness and nicely being.

Empaths might also additionally have a difficult time forming intimate romantic relationships. Some empaths have a worry of having too near with every unique person. They find out that now and again in relationships their middle self is misplaced or subordinated to the emotions, emotions and desires of their intimate accomplice. They have a tough time preserving aside their emotions from their partner's emotions.

Empaths can become emotionally or physical ill from taking in too many emotions or pain from their surroundings. Panic attacks, despair, social tension, fatigue, and continual health issues can all end result from empath overload.

With the proper techniques and way of life in location, empaths can stay on and thrive – and bring their unique and first rate offers to the world.

You are invited to be honest, flexible, and curious – however most of all, be compassionate toward yourself. There may be no flower without the dirt. Practice, take a look at and explore. Your very personal internal voice will will let you apprehend what's running for you.

Here are some factors to take into account as you are making your manner on this adventure:

• You can have a have a look at numerous techniques and mind of thriving as an empath. As excellent as you may, check and discover as you integrate them into your life. Practice and try the strategies extra than as quickly as. Be your very very very own teacher.

• Rough waters will come. Difficult emotions and self-judgment are positive to get up whilst we trade our sorts of conduct.

• If your emotional cup is complete, permit yourself to tug lower lower back and re-have interaction while it feels proper.

Go slow. Show yourself compassion as you are trying to find for growth.

The internal critic can say harsh, merciless topics which you may in no way say to a pal. Be your very own superb pal and allow cross of that voice.

This approach we're able to technique what we're feeling with out pushing it away or defensive without delay to it too tightly. Practice recognition. As Donna Faulds wrote, "love no longer judgment, sows the seeds of tranquility and change."

Chapter 2: Types of Empaths

Knowing you've got empath abilties is the first step to truly apprehend your self. But being an empath can speak with a number of abilities. Knowing which kind of empath, you are especially will help you realise simply what you are able to. Knowing the sort of empath, you are will offer you with more readability and understanding of the arena spherical you. While you may analyze which you are capable of greater than you on the start idea, you'll probably additionally discover that at the quit of this financial disaster, there are some downfalls that encompass owning these abilities.

What Are the Different Types of Empaths?

While empaths can fall into taken into consideration one in all categories, empowered and disempowered, and can also be categorized thru one in every of a type tendencies or characteristics, which encompass empathy or immoderate sensitivity, there are superb varieties of empaths. While all empaths possess the equal capabilities with the intention to revel in what others are feeling and to sense particular energies, empaths can be greater sensitive to fantastic conditions or elements, that is frequently how they're classified.

Emotional Empath

Emotional empaths are a number of the most not unusual and well-known forms of empaths. These are the empaths that absorb the emotional strength from others. They are capable of feel and in reality recognize what each specific man or woman is experiencing emotionally. They are in a characteristic to stroll right into a room and go through a huge wide variety of emotions, relying on the amount of human beings around and counting on what they will be feeling. Emotional empaths just understand if the man or woman they're near is satisfied, sad, disturbing, or pissed off. They are able to select out up on subtle cues, consisting of a trade inside the tone of voice or body language, which many others can't recognize at the same time as a person is trying to cover their right emotions.

Physical Empath

Physical empaths enjoy unique emotions however moreover enjoy their pains as well. These forms of empaths may be by means of or enjoy the identical aches, pains, or signs and symptoms and signs and symptoms that those spherical them can also have. If a bodily empath is inside the presence of a person who is feeling nauseated or has a headache, they'll additionally revel in this nausea or headache. Empaths who can understand what is causing any other individual ache are able to help choose out the numerous symptoms and signs and symptoms they'll be experiencing and may be capable of help them in finding the proper way to heal. Aside from the physical pains, those empaths can experience they'll be furthermore affected by others' strength levels. When they're spherical humans who've low strength degrees or are excessively tired, a physical empath may enjoy their electricity levels turn out to be depleted.

Intellectual Empath

Intellectual empaths have the precise functionality to reflect the language or verbal exchange style of others. These styles of empaths find it clean to speak with humans from numerous backgrounds, cultures, and upbringing. Intellectual empaths will brief choose out up on the best jargon, slang, and accents of others, which allows them to talk on a more private and relatable degree to every new man or woman they meet.

Intuitive Empath

Intuitive empaths also are famous types of empaths. These forms of empath private a heightened revel in of in truth knowledge. Empaths with this intuitive potential are very perceptive of others and their surroundings. They can without trouble spot a lie on the identical time as a person is talking and can discover people with hidden intentions. On pinnacle of this intuitive capacity, masses of those forms of empaths have a eager experience of know-how what's going to appear. Some might also additionally additionally have desires that screen an occasion an incredible manner to occur, or they may be able to pick up on cues from people round them or their environment to have a look at even as some component is ready to get up, along with being capable of sense a heightened anxiety in a room between individuals just in advance than a war of words or argument erupts. Intuitive empaths do no longer truly understand what others are feeling, however they are capable of grow to be aware about, in most cases, the reasoning within the lower returned of those feelings.

Animal Empath

Animal empaths obtained recognition inside the media with fact suggests that centered on individuals who had been able to tame the most behaviorally hard dogs and wild horses. These sorts of empaths are capable of recognize what or how an animal is feeling. This enables them understand what this particular animal desires so that you can assist it heal or to assist tame its erratic conduct. Animal empaths hook up with animals on a deeper stage than most distinctive human beings, and animals commonly have a tendency to gravitate towards them as properly. These kinds of empaths will frequently searching for out the enterprise of animals over that of humans.

Plant Empath

Where animal empaths enjoy a sturdy connection to animals, plant empaths experience this shape of reference to nature and flowers. Plant empaths obviously have a actually green thumb and simply apprehend the manner to properly cope with diverse plants, so they thrive of their environment. Aside from this natural understanding, plant empaths also are capable of better apprehend the houses of particular plants. They can with out troubles understand which plant life are appropriate for ingesting and have healing houses and fantastic abilties they're able to serve. Plant empaths are especially in song with the surroundings and could regularly discover strategies to make certain that plants boom in great environments to meet their dreams. They are capable of understand the best stability of daytime, water, nutrients, and extra for severa flora that permits you to make certain they broaden in ultimate settings.

Environmental Empath/Geomantic Empath

Environmental, geomantic, and psychometric empaths are a completely precise capability to revel in what has occurred or may additionally moreover take area within the location round them. They are also capable to accumulate facts via the usage of the use of touching gadgets in a room to recognize greater approximately what occurred there or to study more approximately the individuals who formerly owned these gadgets. These forms of empaths have a heightened intuition of locations, environments, and gadgets.

Spiritual Empath

Better understood as medium empaths, religious empaths have a deep connection to the religious international. They frequently find out themselves feeling connections to the ones who've died or extraordinary non secular beings. They can't most effective experience on the same time as there are spirits around them but can feel the emotions and bodily ailments of those beings. Spiritual empaths can also speak with those non secular beings. They recognize the ones who have surpassed actually as an emotional is familiar with oldsters which is probably living.

Heyoka Empath

Heyoka empaths are regular in Native American lifestyle, in which they may be defined as a trickster, or heyoka. This kind of empath is often believed to reason problem with their capacity to transport from the bodily global to the spiritual global. They are regularly mediums who're succesful to speak with the ones from the spiritual worlds and relay messages from the bodily worldwide and vice versa. Their specific abilties allow them to show individuals what they need to understand about themselves as a manner to change in a greater extraordinary way.

Useful Abilities of Different Empaths

Psychic Abilities

Some empaths have psychic competencies. Environmental, bodily/medical, animal, plant, and intuitive empaths all very own psychic competencies to a few diploma. This unique type of capability is going beyond surely sensing what those round an empath goes through. Empaths with psychic capabilities can often experience what will appear to someone no matter being miles far from them. They will regularly be hit abruptly with a flood of sensations that indicators them approximately what a person else is going via irrespective of the reality that they'll be nowhere near this person. An empath's heightened senses and excessive levels of empathy can result in them growing psychic abilties or a 6th experience. Empaths who skip without delay to extend their empath gift also can moreover find out that their psychic abilties come out extra simply. Visions

The heightened revel in of an empath lets in them to take a look at topics from a completely unique perspective. They are able to recognition on the finer details of a scenario or individual so that it will in truth recognize what is going on spherical them and inside the different person's life. This functionality permits them to music out the alternative noise that permits you to discover a deeper which means that and finding the critical detail factors that need one's hobby. Not all empaths are able to amplify this ability to its fullest while advanced, and if an empath does enlarge this capacity however lacks the expertise of a manner to nicely positioned it to use, they placed themselves at a extra danger of being taken benefit of.

Intuition

Everybody has a few diploma of their personal intuition, but much like the whole thing else, an empath has a stronger popularity or instinct. When an empath has a robust experience of self, they may be capable of increase their intuitive talents in reality. While intuitive empaths virtually have this capacity, superb empaths can tap into their instinct as nicely. This instinct can assist manual an empath and permits them to better address advantageous situations. With this potential, empaths are able to diffuse terrible conditions in advance than they arise, and this capacity furthermore lets in them to have better judgments about humans.

An empath's intuition is sort of in no way wrong. Only while an empath lacks the self-appreciate and be given as true with in themselves will their instinct be off. For this cause, it's far crucial for an empath to gain a better knowledge of all their abilties and unique tendencies to better employ their intuitive abilties.

Telepathy

This is an capability that some empaths are able to support. Telepathic abilties allow empaths to absolutely apprehend the mind of a few other person. This allows them apprehend exactly in which emotional responses are coming from. Many empaths use this capability to in addition help an man or woman heal and recognize their very very own belief patterns that motive them to have poor or satisfactory emotional responses.

Natural Healing

An empath's capacity to connect with others makes them herbal healers as nicely. Because such a number of humans appear simply to be interested in empaths and sense extra comfortable spherical them, empaths are capable of clearly pay hobby and apprehend what an man or woman needs on the way to heal. While bodily empaths can be capable of heal people on a one-of-a-type level, through being able to proportion what changes they want to make to get over an contamination or fitness circumstance, all empaths are able to do that to a few numerous degree.

Seeing through Lies

Empaths can without issues choose out up on even as a person is dishonest. Whether the phrases you're pronouncing are a lie or the way you present yourself to others is overlaying who you absolutely are, an empath is aware of you're mendacity. Some empaths also can even find out what you're mendacity approximately. Empaths usually have a tendency to avoid humans they comprehend to be dishonest as the ones people will be inclined to provide off horrible energies and, therefore, can depart an empath feeling ill or rather fatigued.

Heightened Senses

Empaths are effortlessly overstimulated due to their heightened senses. This is why an empath prefers to pick out environments which might be calmer and quieter. Bright sun shades, lights, and noise can increase the anxiety that an empath already feels. This heightened sensitivity to outside gadgets can regularly add to the overpowering feeling that empaths struggle to address even as they may be in massive crowds. It is also why they tend to be very cautious approximately in which they paintings, as many artwork environments can cause those senses, making it now not possible for them to be effective.

Creativity

Many empaths have specially contemporary abilities. They will be inclined that allows you to have a take a look at things from a completely precise attitude more effortlessly and may be enormously cutting-edge. For this reason, empaths can also make outstanding a success marketers. Music, art work, and other innovative shops that permit an empath be hands-on are topics they will be willing to thrive at.

Most empaths find out themselves in a few sort of revolutionary agency. This is because of their capability to have a have a study subjects in a different way, think about modern ideas, and feature a deeper feel of being capable of apprehend what's viable— meaning they may take smooth thoughts apart from their very very personal or in collaboration with others and flip those ideas into some issue tangible. Empaths are dreamers, however they do now not in reality honestly dream; they quietly were given all the way down to make their desires a fact.

The Downside of Being an Empath

Empaths may be without trouble manipulated, particularly through oldsters which can be aware about their competencies. When a toxic character, like a narcissist, identifies an empath, they'll try to take advantage of them and take manipulate of them. Empaths obviously lure others, and poor human beings are frequently more inquisitive about an empath than the excellent ones. Due to the being involved and giving nature of an empath, this continues them on consistent protect. While they accept as authentic with their instinct, and masses of can often spot those awful or toxic people, this doesn't positioned a hold on their deep desire to need to help them.

Many empaths typically have a propensity to experience especially insecure about themselves. This insecurity is introduced on not genuinely because of the energy they absorb however because of the fact their abilties are frequently misunderstood. They regularly feel like outsiders and could try and cowl what they will be able to so as to healthy in. Empaths are also humans pleasers. This deep preference to assist every person they come in touch with can result in them having a sufferer mentality or being codependent.

Empaths want their on my own time but additionally tend to retreat or hide in it. They have a hard time fighting with this facade they located on in the front of all people else at the same time as said deep of their nature they have been born to assist others. This is a conflicting level for an empath. It is a stage in which many ignore their abilities and accept a existence they'll be in no manner in reality comfortable with. On the opposite hand, a few discover ways to embody their capabilities and take step one to encompass who they're and what they experience is their reason.

Now you have got a clean statistics of which empath you are. Do you have had been given an improved recognition just humans or are you capable of experience the electricity of various such things as animals and vegetation? Knowing which sort of empath you're will help increase those specific skills that consist of that type of empath. You additionally now recognize what additional talents you probably own as an empath but haven't accessed but. In the following financial disaster, we're capable of cowl the unique way you can enlarge your empathy so that you can begin to stay up on your whole potential.

Chapter 3: The Pros and Cons Of Being An Empath

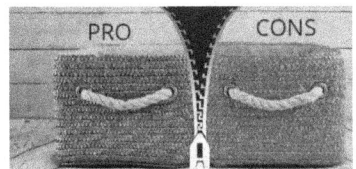

00004.Jpeg

Depending how lengthy you've said that you are an empath, you will be quite acquainted with the professionals and cons of being one. We've already included that one of the downfalls may be the manner it's miles a heavy burden to undergo due to the outside energies and emotions you are surrounded by means of the usage of. However, maximum topics in existence consist of every negatives and positives. The enjoy of feeling the ones emotions round you could be exceptional and useful in plenty of 1-of-a-type methods.

The professionals and cons can't surely be separated as they may be frequently intertwined with each distinctive.

Empaths are listeners. They may be all varieties of pleasure, being outgoing and enthusiastic and typically bubbly. Let's no longer forget the heyoka empath absolutely regarded for being humorous while you least assume it. Their journey can be one in each of emotional bliss, but it is able to furthermore be considered one of emotional turmoil given that empaths may be weighed down with temper swings galore. This is due to the fact their moods aren't normally their very own. If empaths don't actually recognize and differentiate their non-public thoughts and feelings from those of others, they can have fluctuating temper swings that clearly change with the fee of flicking a spark off and off.

As with the fine, being an empath can encompass emotions of despair, tension, panic, worry, and sorrow. Without having any manage over those emotions, you may be experiencing the suffering of others. It's a completely tough problem to need to cope with and shouldn't be finished so on my own.

This is in which compassion is to be had in. An empath have to have at the least one individual they're able to flip to within the throes of those mood swings due to the truth being left on my own can be terrible to intellectual and physical fitness. Find a person, be it a pal or a companion or a member of the family, who you may turn to while things get too overwhelming for you. Whoever you find out, ensure to inform them that all you really need from them is empathic love—the functionality to show compassion with out judging you. This might also additionally help you in restoration from those overwhelming moments.

Most empaths, unless they have prolonged lengthy beyond on their private journeys of self-discovery and self-popularity, don't definitely understand or recognize what's going on within. They don't recognize that they're feeling every different character's feelings like they will be their very very own feelings. This can pretty obviously lead to a myriad of emotions which incorporates confusion, in particular if matters have been grand in a single 2nd and horrible in the next. Understanding their empathic connection is part of the journey.

It's less tough for an empath to withhold their feelings and feelings than it's miles for others. They want to do their awesome not to be barraged by manner of the use of the emotions and feelings of others. In doing so, they regularly grow to be reclusive and learn how to block out those feelings. The drawback of that is that they're able to emerge as bottling up their very non-public emotions or building walls so immoderate that they don't ever allow anybody else in. This can really be terrible for an empath—or every person for that remember quantity—due to the fact the longer you permit the ones feelings and emotions to accumulate inner yourself, the more electricity they build up. Eventually, they could explode and go away in the back of masses of damage to every the empath and those across the empath. This can create an risky surroundings, a intellectual/emotional breakdown, and/or an real illness.

Expressing yourself definitely is a choice, however it's miles a fantastic shape of restoration.

Cons of Being an Empath

Some of these may be counted as professionals relying on the manner you have a look at them. You'll word how short this listing is compared to the list of execs. This is because being an empath is actually a first-rate blessing in case you understand your present nicely.

• You are easily overwhelmed. Wherever there are loads of humans, you'll be overwhelmed with the emotions and emotions emanating off of these that surround you. Sometimes you may be in a room with one man or woman and although feel this way. This is why it's so vital now not to bottle topics up.

• Addictive personalities. Empaths are at risk of seeking out strategies to break out or block out the feelings of others. This manner that they once in a while flip closer to addictive materials together with intercourse, drugs, and alcohol. Learning to guard yourself and your electricity method that you acquired't be struck with the want to break out these things. Instead, you will apprehend the manner to cope with them well.

•   Media may be devastating. Some empaths turn away from media altogether. They can enjoy the emotions of others so strongly that even reading a newspaper is too much for them. It is a harsh global available.

•   Empaths can pick up every highbrow and bodily ailments that others additionally can be troubled through. This can occur even in case you don't come into contact with the other character, relying on how robust your gift is. Needless to mention, no one desires to go through this way.

•   Intuition can be hurtful at the same time as you realize that a person you care about is lying to you or preserving secrets and techniques and strategies from you. The functionality to apprehend and revel in these items can be difficult, especially if you can't show such things. Try to surround yourself with oldsters which is probably properly matched to save you feeling this manner on a ordinary foundation.

• We don't actually have a home. Empaths are herbal wanderers. After a fine quantity of time, we can regularly sense overseas in locations we as quickly as cherished. Our instinct implores with us to discover the super massive worldwide. Due to this, we're now not frequently ever satisfied with one region, however it does endorse we make extremely good tourists.

Pros of Being an Empath

Well, we protected the cons, which I admit have been pretty terrible. Now we get to look at the reasons why being an empath truely is a gift. Bear with me right here, as it's a pretty prolonged listing of motives.

• Empaths are natural healers in lots of high-quality forms: emotional, physical, environmental, animal, you name it. They can use their touch, their voice, and their creativity to accomplish that. Most empaths emerge as on a direction of restoration due to the fact they without a doubt have that pull closer to their career.

• As difficult as crowds can be for an empath, the small circle they frequently turn out to be constructing for themselves is a robust one. Once an empath makes a connection with someone, they're noticeably reliable and loving. We keep onto our cherished ones tightly because of the reality we don't want to allow the high-quality ones bypass.

• Okay, we already recognize this one, but empaths love an insane amount. Their hearts are truely large than most. Being so overloaded with some of these emotions makes faking them hard.

• That intestine instinct is extremely strong and in case you be aware of it, I'm pretty certain you can conquer the arena in case you favored to. Listen to that sixth enjoy of yours because it could save you from functionality risks if it hasn't already.

• Along with having an exceedingly strong sense of intuition, we moreover have brilliant senses. It isn't most effective feelings and feelings which might be heightened. If you find out yourself playing a myriad of sensations with loads extra depth than the ones spherical you, you can chalk that as a splendid deal as being an empath. We have heightened senses that permit us to better revel in our meals, liquids, plants, critical oils, touch, and so on. Admittedly, the ones can every now and then overwhelm us, but they'll furthermore assist save lives. How, you could ask? Well, if you artwork on growing a effective enjoy, along side smell, you will be capable of music down lack of lifestyles or sickness in animals, people, and/or nature.

• I understand we said that the weight of other people's emotions is a burden and we're in reality prone to lows, but we've also were given the other forestall of the spectrum. We have amazing highs, too. Most empaths surely have a deep enthusiasm for life, and at the same time as we're playing it, we revel in pleasure intensely.

• Empaths have an abundance of creativity! We assume and be aware subjects otherwise. Our artwork isn't the simplest revolutionary hassle of our lifestyles, but so are our critiques, conditions, and opportunities. Now, you've probably had the misfortune of being recommended that the manner you consider and/or do matters is inaccurate, but it's a capability all of your very personal. Don't allow all of us take that uncommon creativity faraway from you, and allow it shine brightly rather.

• This Is yet some other con that also seems to be a pro, but we will't be lied to. We are right at reading human beings's thoughts, feelings, and emotions. This approach that we are able to inform at the same time as human beings are mendacity, we will inform on the equal time as people aren't accurate enough, and we can inform while human beings are awful facts.

• Empaths can check emotional and nonverbal cues simply well. It's a talents in numerous places. Due to our accurate senses, we're able to even enjoy the needs of those who do no longer speak, which incorporates animals and vegetation, however additionally the body and infants.

• An empath commonly has a yearning to make the arena a better place. This isn't a preference which you want to ever experience ashamed of. We are capable of bringing masses of excellent changes to this global, and while we will, we want to. There are already too many humans turning blind eyes. Let's paintings on correcting the wrongs occurring round us—together.

• It's particularly important for us to trade the arena thinking about our pull to it. We are youngsters of nature. It's one of the super strategies to de-stress, and it can provide peace and luxury.

• To a few, this might appear extra like a con, however discover that it's pretty cool a exquisite manner to recharge on our non-public. We require a superb diploma of by myself time to get better. It is due to this that we're self-conscious, and anticipate it's brilliant to be self-aware.

How Empaths Can Understand and Help Other People

We've already set up that they're interested in healing and go through the kind of man or woman that needs the arena to be a higher region, but how do they move about making it one? Sure, compassion is a big a part of empathy, however what else can they do? I'd be satisfied to inform you.

The accurate that an empath needs to do—or, as an alternative, is able to doing—is quite depending on what form of empath they'll be. Naturally, pardon the pun, the environmental/geomantic empath has extra of a pull to repair the earth. This is the identical for the plant/flowers empath. When an empath homes their presents, they may use them to hold balance and repair concord into the area. They have their own unique ways of doing this.

Empaths are extraordinary listeners. They in reality care about and experience studying about others, ordinarily due to the fact they may be capable of feel the emotions of the possibility man or woman. There's a kind of rush you experience at the same time as someone tells you their reminiscences as it is able to sense as despite the fact that you have been surely there. When someone dreams assist, an empath can perceive that and provide it hence. The empath can revel in such things as fear or threat, and inside the event that they've strengthened their devices or are attuned to them, they may be able to use the abilties and versions they've developed to take away themselves and others from this sort of situation. They don't communicate about themselves loads, but within the event that they do, it famous that they have got a incredible deal of take delivery of as authentic with inside the person they're sharing with. Often, however, people appear to keep in mind them quickly. This is because of the fact they relate to others of their non-public unique manner.

It is due to this relatability that people sense a pull closer to empaths. It doesn't depend range if the empath is privy to their empathic competencies; human beings will nonetheless be attracted to them. People are inclined to pour their hearts and souls out to empaths who're complete strangers with out always intending to perform that. It takes vicinity on a unconscious degree.

Needless to mention, sometimes the empath goals that release too. That's why it's imperative that they find some of their private kind or they hold the ones specific buddies near. They're terrific people.

Another manner empaths use their capabilities to convey accurate into the region is the potential to resolve troubles. Since they experience learning as hundreds as they do, they've a study many things, and this shows they're constantly sprucing their minds. Sometimes this is a unconscious movement. The empath brings new due to this to the announcing: "Where there can be a will, there may be a manner."

Though it lets in others, you have to be careful of the truth that human beings will frequently need to offload their troubles onto you. These humans won't even realize you. If you don't hold your shield up and improve your power, those problems can convert into being your issues. Make excellent that you preserve the 2 separate. You don't want to be dragged on. Be sincere with your self and others. If a state of affairs looks as if it is going to convey negativity your way, it is adequate to take a step returned and inform the alternative character that you may't deal with it. This is an act of self-maintenance.

I recognize that every now and then it would experience like you are thrown into situations aimlessly and in them, you drink up the feelings of others, however you're stronger than you think. Empaths need to be robust that lets in you to hold each their very very own feelings and the feelings of others. Consider your self a form of strength warrior. You soak up all this electricity and remodel it into some component valuable. You have the functionality to shift the horrific to high-quality. Purify the world. If anybody can do it, an empath can.

Some empaths discover that they need to be in a consistent nation of compassion so as now not to go through adverse effects from outside influences. Others attempt to be as open as they may be, permitting every feeling and sensation to bypass through without an lousy lot have a look at, and in doing so, they release all judgment and try to be as sincere and carefree as feasible. Then there are the empaths who recall in crystal healing to be able to switch and create energetic recovery. The empath who heals the arena in a few element manner they want to is the empath who has a incredible experience of inner peace and balance due to the fact they know that they're following their calling in existence.

If you've already decided what you're supposed to be doing—say, as an instance, mine is releasing my creativity into the arena in any way I deem appropriate—then you definately recognize what I recommend with the resource of feeling a experience of stability. If you're nonetheless searching, don't give up. Follow your instinct and it won't lead you off beam. Bear in thoughts that you may fail some instances. You may think that you've positioned that detail you're supposed to be doing best to comprehend that it changed into not a few aspect greater than a step inside the path of in that you're supposed to be. Keep searching even at the same time as you hit this wall. You are on the adventure you're following for a purpose.

That motive will show itself to you quickly. An empath's gut is commonly right.

Chapter 4: Importance Of Empathy

The living human community lets in us to boom outstanding feelings and moods, further to behaviors that comprise us all and make us act in a one-of-a-type manner in high quality conditions. One of those attitudes is empathy, likely instinctive however that the region we live in these days with its busy tempo greater covers us.

People who are empathetic are higher capable of attraction to, construct and benefit rich and healthful relationships. That is, empathy may be our super high-quality pal in constructing relationships, whether or now not expert or non-public.

Empathy is one of the most essential traits for a a success existence. It is associated with the capacity to have healthy and balanced feelings and to reply properly to each day crises and conflicts, setting up a honest connection with our subordinates, buddies and managers. In a expert environment, empathy allows managers better speak with their group.

Empathy might be very vital for professional development and boom, but care want to be taken not to be overindulged at the same time as we placed ourselves too much in the location of others and feature problem preserving apart non-public and expert lives from the ones of others, our subordinates, and friends.

As with all our skills, empathy is in aspect born with us, and in some extraordinary, we examine it, and it is able to be advanced on this way. In elegant, more undertaking-oriented and significantly competitive executives have little empathic functionality at some degree, which hinders their relationships and compromises their results.

An mind-set that has to do with an instinct

As the character is a social being, this is, who's accustomed with the beneficial aid of nature to stay with particular friends, lifestyles as a whole is part of the essence that defines us and consequently it is very difficult or almost no longer possible to stay without a doubt isolated and far flung of all civilization.

In this coexistence, different behaviors stand up which might be moreover inherent to human wonderful, and that may be from the maximum realistic and supportive or egocentric and evil. Among them, we discover empathy, that exceptional that makes one man or woman feel or get excited on the struggling of the opportunity, and understood as a perhaps abstract form of harmony, empathy is what lets in us to revel in that every different person is not nicely and consequently, to revel in that struggling in our body and soul, act to assist that character to transport beforehand or At least comfort her.

In order to better recognize why there's empathy in someone, it's miles thrilling to note that it has to do with the capability to boom effective ranges of emotional intelligence, which makes us touchy and permeable to struggling every our very own and others.

While there are parents which can be knowledgeable and raised with out the slightest hobby in developing emotional intelligence but probable cognitive, there are also people who because of the way wherein they were raised or even lived reviews, have a immoderate sensitivity inside the path of what takes place to others and consequently they display more empathy in situations of pain or struggling.

Why Is It Necessary to Be Empathic with Our Peers?

We all understand that the societies in which we stay lead us to be quite individualistic beings, greater concerned with our very non-public correct than with the community proper.

However, it's miles crucial that empathy becomes a common and regular mind-set amongst us because of the fact so that it will rely on the nicely-being of a community. This is because of the reality being supportive, paying attention to the other, accompanying him in his struggling or assisting him is what makes us human and enriches us as humans.

The following are the importance of being empathic that is implemented straight away to normal life:

- Solidarity:

It is wrong to think that this word is immediately related excellent to volunteer artwork. Looking at others understanding your difficulties and imparting help when you want it, and even as you can, is a precious way to expose concord. So do now not near your eyes to your buddies, family and coworkers who need your help for some cause.

- Respect:

Understanding that each one chooses the route they need for existence and respecting this decision is essential for any character. Unfortunately, this isn't always what continuously takes region within the worldwide, but it isn't because of this that you may not act politely and kindly to everyone. Respect the way of life picks, religion, sexual orientation, political opinion, and such hundreds of first-rate topics that may cause problems in communicate. If older humans didn't query what's unique approximately them, the arena might be dwelling extra harmoniously in recent times.

- Listen to The Essence:

Empathy teaches how essential it's miles to pay attention to humans in essence. This manner which you pay attention to what the opportunity has to mention, assimilate, take transport of and supply your opinion respectfully. This sort of behavior demonstrates that you are involved about getting every body's opinion expressed in due vicinity. This behavior is crucial for a healthful debate, is not it?

- Learning:

It is crucial which you are constantly evolving sooner or later of your lifestyles. For this, it's far critical that you do no longer prevent analyzing. Sharing records with one-of-a-type specialists, discussing healthily, reading, analyzing and pursuing complementary courses and training are all techniques to keep you updated and evolve regularly. So in no way overlook about to invest in your continuing education and special methods of studying.

- Collectivity:

Collective cognizance will be very crucial in organization environments in addition to outside, as this is vital for a superb coexistence in society. Much more than really knowledge a manner to paintings in businesses, the community teaches to recognize each special's reviews and to embody everyone, even those who have had fewer possibilities.

Did you apprehend all this significance of being an empathic person? If you did not recognize approximately them but, you are now entire of treasured expertise to use to your each day existence. Be wonderful to demonstrate your high-quality trends related to the factors we communicate approximately up proper right here. In addition to being vital in your intellectual well-being, the ones gadgets are vital for particular social coexistence outdoor and in the organization environment.

Besides, people are social beings, and therefore in the long run all of us is probably in contact with one of a kind people. And just within the ones moments, empathy may be very critical for severa motives: Empathy Facilitates Communication

Empathic humans can empathize with their opposite numbers and consequently extra without issues apprehend what their counterpart goals to talk. Of route, it although subjects how exactly the opposite man or woman expresses and the manner exactly he communicates what he desires to bring. In precept, however, it is crucial to correctly apprehend and try to apprehend the opportunity character a good way to assure clean communique. As a result, misunderstandings may be avoided, which permits in every the non-public and the expert surroundings.

Empathy Creates Harmonious Relationships

Empathy is specially crucial in friendships, partnerships or own family relationships due to the fact, in the end, real relationships can best be tough without mutual facts. Especially in battle conditions, empathy can save you a extraordinary struggle from breaking out.

Empathic human beings are able to understand their opposite numbers, and that is the first step already carried out. In the subsequent step, it's miles crucial to simply accept the attitudes and perspectives of the other character - but that is going beyond empathy. A warfare might be solved very without problems if all men and women concerned not handiest of their non-public feature but additionally in the exclusive. Conflict situations can frequently boom if too many feelings are involved, so it's miles beneficial to limit oneself to cognitive empathy in such situations.

Empathy should have an impact on relationships no longer best in conflict conditions but in huge. For who makes use of his empathy capability to get to understand his fellow people better and higher, can see how his fellow human beings tick. What quirks does my counterpart have? How can I please my counterpart? What have to I keep away from in order now not to disenchanted my counterpart? All of those questions can be responded by using the use of empathic humans little by little, thereby enabling a harmonious amassing together.

Self-Reflection Empathy

If you're empathetic and honest with yourself, then you definitely truly have already got important trends to reflect on your self. Because empathy can be beneficial no longer most effective in contact with others but furthermore in contact with oneself. Become aware of what mind or emotions you have got yourself and ask why this is the case. Have an facts of your very very own mistakes and quirks. Do not without a doubt count on negatively however also allow compliments.

Observe yourself even in conflict situations. Try to undergo life with a immoderate level of mindfulness so that you can understand extra. Through empathy and mindfulness, you could alternate and growth yourself.

Thus, empathy helps you to have interaction with specific people and with yourself to understand and decorate your attitudes and feelings and is therefore very critical to every body. To whole the idea, demonstrating the ones virtues complements your private advertising and marketing and marketing within the short, medium and long term. This is due to the fact all other experts will see how hundreds you are committed to enhancing your profession and others.

Also, it is essential to have nice relationships with third activities; expand more respectful and healthy relationships with pals, colleagues and coworkers. It is especially crucial to apply empathy with the nearest family which include parents, siblings and companions. From empathy, we see that in any area of every day existence, we are able to generate greater healthy relationships with 1/three occasions.

Somehow, empathy moreover gives us the possibility to get to recognize ourselves extra. This is because it requires clean emotional expertise and emotional vocabulary; generated via that know-how of our reactions on an emotional degree in numerous situations. This leads us to higher apprehend emotions in others; and use this understanding to have the capability to speak with others, placing ourselves within the vicinity of the other.

Knowing this, and the whole thing this is recognized about empathy, I encourage you to start the usage of empathy to your conversations, and you could see how you enhance your dating with others.

What Are the Strengths of Empathic Leadership?

Combined with technical abilities, ability to influence through example, creativity and particular communique, empathy completes a package deal deal of necessities that pinnacle control need to-have. Of course, not all managers can acquire this degree, but it's miles critical that they are trying to bring those traits to life in an assertive manner.

Imagine a pacesetter who does now not have the capacity to have a examine his fanatics and apprehend their expert and personal problems and help them. Another awful scenario is when a manager who cannot make the organization is continuously evolving due to the fact he can be very worried about his position.

The above examples come close to selfishness, do not they? For that is what loss of empathy can create. An empathetic leader is worried with seeing every group in my view, respecting their professional and private variations and taking this beneath attention at the same time as delegating needs. In addition, it's far much less tough to hold effective and innovative recommendation to humans in detrimental conditions.

Have you had empathic manage? Unfortunately, we are not generally fortunate. However, you can try to be the empathic chief of the future. Through effective equipment, the technique teaches extra about your self, emotional intelligence, self-self belief, humanized management, behavioral fashion identity, and masses of various factors of interest to benefit effective and private and expert normal overall performance.

What Do You Need to Know About the Pros and Cons of Empathy?

The without a doubt furnished reasons why empathy will be very important to people also represent the principle benefits of empathy. Empathy brings with it the best benefits even as you hook up with one of a kind humans. Empathy People are characterised via using knowledge, compassion and helpfulness. In the private sphere, conflicts can be avoided, and relationships may be progressed.

In addition, empathetic humans are normally very sympathetic to one-of-a-kind human beings, due to the fact they display pretty some information. In the expert surroundings, you could use empathy to beautify conversation in conjunction with your colleagues, employees or supervisors. You also can boom your personal power of persuasion because of the fact you understand the way high-quality movements and phrases have an effect on others. You can use this in negotiations.

The most effective drawback of empathy is placed even as human beings cannot demarcate sufficient. In many locations, it is crucial no longer to permit oneself be carried away by using using the use of the feelings of various human beings or even confused with them.

If the quantity of empathy is sincerely too excessive, it is viable that one's very very very own attitudes and feelings will take a once more seat, placing one's very own dreams in the again of. In addition, there is a threat that empathic humans may be exploited. If you're privy to the ones hazards, you can keep away from them thru reading to mention NO. If your private feelings and goals come first, then your empathy will not have an impact on you negatively.

How Can Empathy Be Promoted?

Especially in adulthood, human beings lose the capability to empathize with others. Over time, they can not understand and recognize their very non-public thoughts and feelings or the ones of others. With some clean sporting sports, you could enjoy empathy or empathy all over again.

- Learn Empathy

Empathy can't be magnified from at some point to the following. The pinnacle data is that every guy or girls has the prevailing of being an empathic individual. If you agree with you studied empathy with yourself, then it's far surely simplest a determinate, constrained empathy that can change you to a immoderate diploma of empathy. Empathy is like many distinctive abilities: workout makes quality. To sell your empathy, use the following 3 practices in normal life, and you may soon realise just how empathetic it is.

- Perception

In order to sell one's very non-public empathy, it's miles crucial to understand the opportunity person exactly. Listen cautiously, paying interest no longer handiest to what is stated but moreover to facial expressions and gestures. Often it's miles trifles that display what others assume and revel in. For example, does a person chuckle collectively along together with his mouth and no longer together with his eyes? Do the person's moves suit what they're pronouncing? Be aware of what your fellow human beings are doing and try to come to be aware about the mind behind the movement. Do it your self - what do you agree with you studied and experience in high-quality situations?

- Questioning

It isn't commonly feasible to find out the thoughts and emotions of others via pure notion. Facial expressions, gestures and frame language, in standard, are awesome in one in every of a type humans. So without a doubt ask if you do not apprehend your counterpart. How are you feeling proper now? What do you think about it? - through such questions, you may check what goes on in your counterpart and at the equal time, develop a extra sizable conversation.

- Leading with the resource of Example

Empathy regularly has a few issue to do with whether or no longer or now not your counterpart opens as masses as you. So set an excellent example and speak about your mind, feelings and views yourself. By doing so, you can get to understand yourself higher and lead your fellow people to open up.

With those carrying occasions, you step by step amplify a revel in of what others assume and enjoy, thereby developing your empathy.

- Empathy in Children

If you're questioning the manner to beautify your children's empathy, then rest assured: Children take a look at empathy through the usage of manner of themselves if you permit them to. Especially with very more youthful youngsters, they do not recognize everything round them but though, recognize and empathize with emotions. As a quit quit result, they manifestly boom empathy. So ensure which you do no longer suppress such empathic reactions.

If your children are speakme about thoughts or sensations, then attempt to listen attentively and respond. In maturity, there is usually a loss of empathy due to the truth humans themselves prevent taking note of their very personal thoughts and sensations and therefore are not open to the mind and emotions of others. Therefore, help no longer only your children however moreover your fellow people.

Many professionals consider empathy as a congenital assets that is genetically determined. The life enjoy of an person can most effective enhance or weaken it. Empathy is based upon on the availability and richness of lifestyles enjoy, the accuracy of perception, the ability to music in, listening to the interlocutor, at the identical emotional wave with him.

Various schooling techniques assist to boom empathic skills (situation to their innate presence), boom the capacity to use empathy in personal and professional verbal exchange more correctly.

Teach Your Children Empathy

Children have an innate capability to empathize. They are obviously able to empathize with someone else's ache and unhappiness - whether or not or not it comes from different kids or pets. As the child grows and develops, a unusual internal conflict starts - empathy competes with childish egoism and undeveloped power of thoughts.

Children are able to learn how to be affected character and take into account others if dad and mom will help them develop those developments. Most human beings have witnessed tantrums that kids roll up at the same time as they're worn-out, hungry, uncomfortable, or at the same time as they may be not given what they want and aren't allowed to do what they need. Over time, they discover ways to tolerate such dissatisfaction higher.

It can be very critical to train children to be tolerant and empathize with others. We, adults, must set an instance for them, because of the truth children particularly have a look at via imitation of dad and mom and exclusive household. We check compassion all our lives, and dad and mom need to begin talking approximately this with their toddler as quickly as feasible. In these conversations, it's miles critical now not to keep away from tough problems and to talk about person variations brazenly.

Children are very curious and regularly ask such questions on people, things, approximately the arena that adults are surprised: why did the kid even think about this? The way children specific their emotions, react to warfare conditions, and one-of-a-kind people's reviews in big component depend on their temperament.

How to Teach Your Children Empathy?

1.Encourage their interest and ardour for exploring the location.

2.Teach them to attend to others and themselves.

three.Do now not domesticate selfishness and spoilage in them, do not inspire rudeness.

four.By your example, display them how to expose sensitivity, care, empathy.

five.Refuse double necessities: do not deal with some organizations of human beings in some other way than others.

6.Teach you methods to narrate to errors: provide an reason behind that errors are inevitable; they need to be diagnosed, take responsibility and apologize. If you are making a mistake, display the proper response through example.

7.Make superb they agree to the recommendations. Clearly set up, unchanging limits assist kids apprehend how their behavior and misconduct have an effect on others.

8.Pay attention to situations at the same time as kids show kindness and sympathy, praise them. For instance, I appreciated which you helped a friend address the wound even as it fell.

nine.Encourage the choice in kids to help others.

10.   Wean them to grasp on other labels and talk badly approximately people.

eleven.   Do not depart beside the point conduct unpunished.

As they grow old, children will start to understand the importance and charge of compassion better, mainly within the event that they participate in charity or volunteer sports. Compassion allows to increase other essential non-public competencies in order to be beneficial to the kid at the same time as he grows up, and further, will assist him to deal with others extra tolerantly.

You are Next!

Now the following step is to apply all your career and private expertise intelligently. But do no longer hesitate to test similarly. Look for extra content material fabric and guides that could surely contribute on your education as someone and expert.

It's essential which you charge this form of proactivity in your element and even though inspire it from others. It's no better whilst surely anyone who lives with you wants to be the amazing model they'll be.

Chapter 5: Understanding Your Empathic Nature

Empathy performs a key feature inside the functioning of society. It promotes our desires, sharing critiques, and dreams amongst humans. Our neural networks are set up to connect with the neural structures of others to every see and understand their emotions and to separate them from our non-public, which makes it feasible for humans to live with each special with out always struggling with.

Empathy is pretty critical because it allows us be able to comprehend and apprehend the emotions distinct people are going via so that we may be capable of respond efficiently to their situations reachable. To a extra quantity, it's been related to the social behaviors with research supporting it, arguing that the extra empathy then, the greater one has a bent to help. Notably, an empath also may be capable of inhibit social moves or possibly visit the volume of getting an amoral behavior. For example, a person who sees a car twist of destiny and is beaten thru emotions witnessing the sufferer in severe ache might be a bargain much less in all likelihood to help that man or woman.

Importantly, having strong empathy can also bring about terrible motives. Such strong feelings towards our own family individuals; social or racial organizations can reason hatred between one another brought about via loss of self assurance. Also, oldsters which can be professional in analyzing different human beings's feelings can begin using this possibility for their very very own profits by using deceiving the sufferers. They encompass the manipulators, fortune tellers, and psychics.

Interestingly, human beings with higher psychopathic inclinations display extra utilitarian responses in events in which there are moral dilemmas, like, footbridge issues. In this test, people need to decide whether or not or no longer to push someone off a bridge to stop a train approximately to kill five others laying on the song.

Measuring Empathy

Quite frequently, a self-report questionnaire is used in measuring empathy. Such styles of questionnaires consist of the Interpersonal Reactivity Index (IRI) or Questionnaire for Cognitive and Affective Empathy (QCAE). In the approach of measuring empathy, the person is requested to indicate how a brilliant deal they take shipping of the statements which can be set to assist measure the special varieties of empathy that one might be having.

One will discover statements like, "It affects me very loads whilst genuinely one of my buddies is dissatisfied," which QCAE test makes use of to degree the effect of empathy. QCAE performs a key characteristic inside the identification of cognitive empathy via the use of statements which encompass "I try and have a study every body's problem of a battle of phrases earlier than I make a preference."

With the use of this approach, it became determined that humans scoring higher on affective empathy have extra grey count wide variety. Grey depend amount is stated to be a set of nerve cells in the anterior insula, that is an area of the thoughts.

This location is frequently related to directing incredible and terrible emotions by using manner of coordinating ecological stimulants—for example, seeing an automobile crash with instinctive and programmed in essence sensations. Likewise, human beings utilising this technique to gauge compassion determined that excessive scorers of sympathy had a frequently dark location in the dorsomedial prefrontal cortex.

The activation of this precise place takes region at the same time as there are extra cognitive procedures, and this included the Theory of Mind. The principle is the capability of 1 to function the highbrow ideals to oneself and every one of a kind character. The idea also accepts the truth that one has to understand that the alternative individual has desires, ideals, intentions, and views one among a kind from theirs.

Can Humans Lack Empathy?

Several instances have established that not absolutely everyone have empathy. For example, on foot down Minnesota, you encounter a homeless individual shivering inside the cold. You will phrase that few people will specific sympathy, empathy, or compassion for the homeless individual. Most of the time, we've got were given visible human beings expressing outright hostility closer to such human beings. So, what is probably the motive people expressing empathy selectively? Various elements expect the function. How we see the alternative individual, how we characterize their practices, what we fault for the opportunity individual's difficulty, and our very very non-public past encounters and desires all emerge as an imperative trouble.

Further, I definitely have come to find out that there are number one matters that make a contribution to humans experiencing empathy— and people are socialization and genetics. Going lower back to age and time, we get to understand that our dad and mom have the genes that quite make a contribution to personalities, and this includes our propensity within the path of topics, empathy, sympathy, and compassion. Notably, our parents spent sufficient time with us socializing, we chat with peers, the society, and the network at huge and that is sufficient to affect us. The interactions have loads to do with how we cope with others, our emotions, and ideals as they'll be a mirrored photo of our values and ideals instilled in us while on the early ranges of existence.

Reasons Why People Lack Empathy:

1.   We dehumanize sufferers

Quite often, we're trapped in the idea that folks that are specific from us have excellent behaviors and feelings from us. This is obvious even as handling individuals who are precise from us. A precise example is a time even as we watch conflicts, fights, disagreements, and calamities from a distant places land. Then, we grow to be having a good deal much less or no empathy with the idea that those struggling are essentially distinctive from us.

2.   We blame victims

It happens that humans start blaming a specific state of affairs or suffering at the sufferer for his or her condition no matter them present device a terrible experience. Many times, people ask what the crime the victim had committed to initiate an assault. This tendency stems from the notion that the world is a sincere and simply area.

We can't brush away the fact that empathy at instances could likely fail, however human beings commonly parent out a manner to find out with others in an collection of instances. This capability to appearance things from a person else's factor of view and find out with another's feelings assumes a super task in our public sports. Sympathy absolutely permits us a top notch manner to take our time and recognize others and compels others to move in advance and take an movement so as to help the individual that is suffering. Empathy is all about minding approximately each different man or woman.

Can Empathy Be Selective?

Previous researchers have located that humans have a tendency to be extra empathetic for participants belonging to their institution, just like those from their ethnic businesses. For example, one researcher checked the cerebrums of Chinese and Caucasian participants at the identical time as they watched recordings of human beings from their ethnic gathering in soreness. They likewise watched human beings from an exchange ethnic accumulating in torment.

A look at via using one in every of a type researchers has moreover located that thoughts regions involved in empathy are quite tons less energetic whilst we're looking people present technique ache for acting unfairly. When a person is looking a rival sports institution failing, we can be capable of see activation within the thoughts areas that are concerned in the subjective pride.

It is good to phrase that during such times, we in no way sense empathy for the people who are not of our employer. When giving rewards to contributors who are not in our institution, the mind worried in such hobby have become very lively while worthwhile the equal ethnic organization, but at the same time as looking people of various organizations being harm, the thoughts activeness remains equal.

At times, it's miles in reality useful to be a good deal much less empathetic to be successful. To positioned this into mindset, on the same time as in a warfare, a soldier ought to have a great deal less empathy, in particular towards the enemy who might in all likelihood need to kill them. From the motive, it emanates that people tend to have an implicated mind while they may be harming others and have a less energetic thoughts if the act is justified.

Assessing If You Are an Empath

Here is a easy check that will let you apprehend whether or not or no longer or now not you're an empath or not. Go through it, imparting a simple positive or no method to each query.

•   Have I at any time been categorized as touchy, introvert, or shy?

•   Do I get demanding or beaten regularly?

•   Do fights, yelling, and arguments often make me ill?

•   Do I regularly have the sensation that I don't healthy in?

•   Do I find out myself being tired through the crowds, and by means of way of that then do I within the important need my time on my own so you can repair myself?

•   Do odors, noise, or nonstop talkers get me beaten?

•   Do I clearly have chemical sensitiveness or low tolerance for scratchy clothes?

•   Do I pick out using my automobile whilst attending an occasion or going to an area simply so I is probably free to depart in advance?

- Do I use food as my deliver to break out from stress?

- Do I experience scared of being suffocated with the beneficial useful resource of courting intimacy?

- Do I without troubles startle?

- Do I virtually have a sturdy response to medicinal drugs or caffeine?

- Do I in reality have a low threshold for ache?

- Do I have a tendency to be socially isolated?

- Do I get to soak up the stress, signs and signs and symptoms, and emotions of the alternative human beings?

- Am I in general crushed thru doing numerous matters at a move, and do I continually choose managing one hassle at a cross?

- Do I top off myself generally?

• Do I want a long time to get higher after being with difficult humans or energy vampires?

• Do I continually revel in being in a higher location at the same time as in small towns than the massive ones?

• Do I constantly select having one on one interplay and small corporations and now not the massive collecting?

You can now try to comprehend who you're by calculating your effects.

• If you agreed to at least five of the questions, then you definitely are in part an empath.

• If you agreed to at least ten questions, you are at a moderate degree.

• If you agreed to eleven or fifteen questions, you then without a doubt are a robust empath with sturdy dispositions.

• If you have agreed to greater than fifteen questions, then it's definitely that you are a entire-blown empath.

The power of will of your degree of an empath is essential because it will make it easy so that you could make clear the sorts of needs and the sort of strategy you will need to comply in a piece a extremely good manner to satisfy them. With the electricity of will, then you'll be capable of find out a comfort area for your life.

What Areas Does It Affect Our Lives?

Being an empath is a few element that affects every location of your existence. It's now not like a method wherein you clock in, do your artwork, clock out and go domestic. The experience of being an empath is one that takes vicinity 24 hours an afternoon, 7 days according to week. Subsequently, there may be no place of your lifestyles that is left unaffected via your empathic capabilities. Although you may't save you your empathic nature from influencing your existence you may manipulate those influences, thereby taking control from the outcomes of your emotional surroundings.

Health

One of the most not unusual regions stricken by empathic abilities is someone's fitness. The terrible results of the regular bombardment of feelings may be overwhelming at quality and devastating at worst. Although these consequences can not be averted altogether while someone is aware of them they may be capable of make alternatives and choices that better guard their health.

Some of the lesser physical signs and symptoms that empaths frequently be afflicted by consist of complications, fatigue and minor panic assaults. These are generally introduced on with the aid of prolonged exposure to big crowds, noisy environments or every other situation associated with harsh sensory input. Such signs and symptoms fade quick once the empath finds a quiet location in which to rebalance their energies. In the event that they can't escape, those signs can turn out to be more excessive paperwork, consisting of migraine, dizziness, nausea or maybe muscle ache.

In addition to affecting bodily fitness and health, empathic abilties can substantially have an effect on someone's emotional fitness and properly being as properly. Lesser symptoms and signs and symptoms embody a notable feeling of disappointment, low electricity ranges or even slight stress and tension. Such signs and symptoms are typically the result of being in a awful environment or round humans with negatively charged feelings. They also can be the quit end result of becoming emotionally spent due to supporting those in want. If left unchecked, those signs and symptoms can trade into more severe problems, along with despair, immoderate anxiety or even rage in a few times. Needless to say, it is important which you find out a place of solitude inside the event which you start experiencing any of these signs and symptoms and signs, as simplest then are you able to begin to undo the harmful effects of your surroundings. Daily

meditation may also help to growth your stamina in incredibly charged emotional environments.

Addictions

Many empaths find the ordinary go with the flow of emotional power that bombards their senses hard to address every now and then. While most discover wholesome tactics to cope with those conditions others flip to a lot much less wholesome strategies. In fact, some expand addictions in their quest to stupid their senses and convey a feel of tranquility to their minds. While some addictions are a bargain a good deal much less risky than others, the bottom line is that no addiction is absolutely healthful. Therefore, it is essential that you be seeking out addictive conduct on your existence that permits you to avoid any long-time period, dangerous effects.

One such addiction is consuming. This makes a number of revel in on the identical time as you maintain in thoughts the results meals must have on each the body and the mind. Most consuming addictions involve treats or comfort food, matters that make a person happy simply thinking about them. Thus, now not excellent do meals including ice cream and cake offer a short enhance of sugary energy, similarly they create a enjoy of consolation and peace that facilitates to restore the mind. From time to time such an indulgence may be healthy, however, whilst that indulgence becomes addiction it is able to have very horrific consequences on each frame and mind.

Other addictions include consuming alcohol and smoking. These addictions additionally make revel in seeing as they offer a chemical depressant that enables to stupid an empath's senses, thereby relieving them from the inner chaos and turmoil that their thoughts testimonies most of the time. Shopping is a few other commonplace dependancy, one that is less understood than the others. However, it makes first-rate experience whilst you take the time to actually consider it. When a person shops they have the wish and expectation of locating some thing so that you can deliver delight and success to their lives. Since empaths often be bothered by way of disappointment or maybe melancholy, such an expectation will pass a long way to elevating their spirits. In the stop, those addictions are typically nothing greater than an empath's way of self-medicating via their greater vital bouts of despair and tension.

If you enjoy such addictive conduct it is crucial to speak to someone who is probably succesful to help you conquer it. Alternatively, turning to things like meditation and exercise in region of addictive conduct can in fact assist replace volatile behavior with more healthy, extra beneficial ones. Relationships, Love, and Sex

Unfortunately, the empathic nature of someone regularly outcomes in them finding themselves inside the midst of poisonous relationships that they in fact can not escape. This dynamic has critical motives. First, empaths are generally drawn to folks that need help, seeing as they have got an inherent want to offer assist and assist on every occasion possible. While this seems like a wonderful aspect, the truth is that it can bring about empaths being interested in folks that are abusive or maybe self-detrimental in nature. The more damaged someone, the greater appealing they are to an empath. The 2nd cause is that an empath can't abandon someone in want. Therefore, even supposing they apprehend their dating is poisonous they grow to be caught as they cannot supply themselves to cause suffering to the alternative character through finishing the relationship. Talking to a person, be it a pal or a counselor, can go an extended way to resolving this seize 22 scenario.

Another way that empaths conflict with relationships is that they will be often emotionally spent, which means that they don't continuously have the power had to nurture a wholesome and loving courting. This doesn't propose that empaths don't crave deep and significant relationships, as an opportunity they don't commonly reserve sufficient emotional energy to put money into their very very own happiness, spending all of it at the happiness of others as a substitute. The handiest real technique to this is for an empath to discover someone who's each very energetic further to very information regarding the empath's plight.

Love and intercourse are also tremendously impacted with the resource of way of someone's empathic abilities. While many human beings see sex as an act that expresses love amongst humans, empaths regularly see it as a manner to deaden their senses, restoring them to a state of being bodily grounded. This can purpose tension in any courting wherein the opportunity man or woman feels greater lusted after than loved close to intimacy. The fact of the problem is that empaths will in no manner have interaction in an intimate come across with all of us who they don't love deeply, consequently any intimate hobby will continuously be finished out of affection irrespective of outward appearances. The crucial thing for any empath is to make sure they screen their love for his or her accomplice on a normal foundation via any way possible.

Parenting

Parenting is a tough sufficient revel in on its very own, now not to say at the same time as it entails an empath at one prevent or the opportunity. Even so, each empath alive has grown up as a little one with empathic abilities, and countless empaths begin families in their personal, for this reason stepping into the world of being a figure with empathic talents. The growth of emotional recognition between parents and children may be every a blessing and a curse. It is therefore essential that you turn out to be privy to the risks so you can higher manage the effects of your empathic skills inside your family relationships.

As a determine you can conflict with the glide of emotional enter you get preserve of out of your youngsters. This is made worse via the reality that youngsters are normally complete of conflicting and hard emotions because of the biochemical modifications their our bodies are constantly going thru. Needless to say, this handiest serves to boom the chaotic nature of the emotional input, developing a in no way finishing whirlwind for your thoughts. It is critical which you increase the functionality to detach from emotional enter with a purpose to shield your self from turning into certainly unhinged due to such heightened emotional stimuli. Practicing yoga or meditation on a every day basis can assist make all the distinction.

One of the positives of being an empathic figure is that you can experience on the identical time as your children are struggling. This offers you a bonus of being capable of make your self available to them even though they may be trying to cowl their internal turmoil. Taken too some distance, however, this potential can become a shape of privateness invasion, consequently incredible ever use it as a device, in no way as a weapon. If your kids refuse the help you provide you want to respect their privacy and allow them to address their scenario on their very very own.

As a toddler you may find existence virtually extra hard due to your empathic abilities. Every toddler does topics that they remorse, subjects that often reason their dad and mom a super amount of ache and distress. However, most youngsters are able to located the ones sports within the returned of them alternatively speedy, transferring directly to higher instances. Unfortunately, your empathic competencies will increase the guilt and sorrow you enjoy for the whole thing that reasons your mother and father any shape of pain. Even the slightest of factors which incorporates a touch white lie can motive you to enjoy clearly guilt ridden due to the truth similarly to feeling your remorse you can also experience the pain your parents revel in at the same time as you mislead them. This is pretty unfair, of path, but it regularly consequences in empaths growing the very high-quality of standards in terms of morals and virtue. Developing emotional detachment, however, is quite advocated to be able to reduce the consequences.

Work

Another environment that can impact an empath in a truely large way is the workplace. This is especially true for any undertaking that creates a considerably aggressive environment. In addition to experiencing their non-public pressure and tension, empaths might also enjoy the strain and tension of those spherical them. This can bring about an empath being ten instances greater forced out than every body else at any given time. Needless to say, this wishes to be avoided the least bit fees.

The first rule for an empath is to create limitations within the administrative center. While the knee-jerk response is to provide assist and solace to those in need, this could show disastrous if no limits are installation. As an empath you want to make certain that you get hundreds of by myself time to balance your energies and recharge your batteries. The heightened emotional environment in the administrative center will drain you faster than each distinctive surroundings, consequently you want to take greater precautions to make certain your non-public fitness and nicely-being.

Perhaps the exquisite case situation is for an empath to find a interest that lets in them to be pretty self enough. Although too much solitude may additionally want to have its downside as properly it could be a higher challenge to stand than that of being continuously mentally crushed and emotionally exhausted. The essential element is to area your desires first commonly at the way to save you from becoming absolutely burned out and now not able to carry out your manner correctly.

Extraordinary Perceptual Abilities

Fortunately, there are various tremendous approaches in which your lifestyles can be appreciably stronger and enriched due to your inherent present. As an empath you can discover you have got high-quality abilities that appear nearly otherworldly at the begin. Rather than doubting or maybe fearing those abilties you want to include them and enlarge them so you gain each benefit that they have to provide.

One hassle many empaths enjoy occasionally is the capability to appearance destiny or a ways off activities. Commonly known as premonitions, these visions can show up pretty unexpectedly, mainly whilst the event would now not impact the empath themselves. If you have ever seen a place or a person honestly on your mind, simplest to look that character or area on the information speedy in a while, you've got got had a premonition. This may not appear all of the time, and no longer all empaths have this ability. However, in case you revel in it you want to encompass it for the miracle that it's far. There likely won't be some component you may do to have an effect at the situation, so do now not enjoy as even though you are by some means obligated to keep the area. Instead, that is simplest a state of affairs wherein your unconscious taps into the collective unconscious and discovers some detail interesting. The quicker you accept as actual with this capacity is, the stronger it becomes.

Enhanced dream states are every different common phenomenon professional with the useful resource of way of empaths. This stands to motive as desires are born of the unconscious, truly as emotions and instinct. Therefore, the stronger your skills of instinct and emotional sensing the more immoderate your goals can be. At the very least you could have an increased ability to take into account your dreams, some element the common character generally lacks. However, the opportunities are your desires can also be richer in detail, extra colorful or maybe longer lasting as properly. Even better, you may experience what are referred to as lucid goals in that you end up aware about the truth which you are dreaming. This opens up an entire new length that allows you to enjoy some factor inside the dream global with the same intensity as although it have been taking place in the actual international.

Finally, there are the ones empaths who have the potential to experience beyond human or non-public enjoy. If you have got got were given ever 'study' the thoughts of an animal, or sensed the needs of a plant you're this form of people. The easy fact is that thoughts and feelings are pure power by using nature, therefore empaths can understand them no matter their basis. After all, a concept is a concept, regardless of whether it comes from someone or a tree. Therefore, it must be in reality as feasible to have a examine the best as it's miles the alternative. Many empaths do not non-public this expertise, but, that does not suggest that their talents are weaker or a whole lot less superior. Rather, it is a rely form of frequency. While a few empaths are genuinely tuned in to the human frequency, others are greater in song with the frequencies of nature. If you sense extra at domestic with nature, and you could feel the dreams of flowers and animals, then this is how your empathic abilties have an effect on your lifestyles.

In the give up, truly absolutely everyone's empathic abilties can have an impact on their lives in exceptional and unique strategies. This is because of the fact each person's competencies are one among a kind, as are the lives they lead. Therefore, what's real for one character isn't usually actual for some specific. As a result the most crucial element you can do is to find out what's proper for you and the strategies that art work great for you in phrases of honing and harnessing your capabilities. The greater on top of things of your talents you're the greater on pinnacle of factors of your existence you turns into. After all, being an empath doesn't want to be complex and difficult, as an alternative it can be some thing absolutely first rate and great.

CHAPTER 6: The Empaths

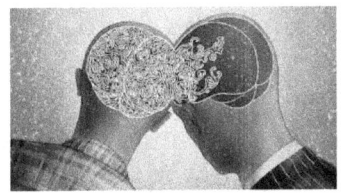

Empaths are folks that will deliver in sure humans's emotions and moods as their private. We come into the area with heightened senses, which can be in addition reinforced via severa obstacles or traumas we've encountered at some point of their lives.

Empaths occupy the entire and a totally opposite issue of the continuum from egocentric, sociopathic or psychopathic guys. Empaths are people that have hooked up coping techniques all through their youth while faced with traumatic situations that artwork into their maturity. We broaden outwardly, deliver-in and empathize with special humans's feelings, which includes their perpetrators. Yet this preference to hold in distinct human beings's emotions isn't terrific to perpetrators. It occurs to in reality every body and all of us and is mainly not unusual in companies or crowds.

Throughout every case, Empaths seem to recognize and maintain on the alternative person's center emotions. This technique is constructed to make certain the Empath considers itself as now not extraordinary from others.

Having an Empath isn't a psychiatric disease; it's far but each other way in which the World shows itself and encounters itself intangible nature from the Oneness element of view.

The want to address emotions that are not genuinely theirs, in spite of the truth that, perhaps burdensome and putting aside for Empaths, contributing to misery, unhappiness, and famous uncertainty over what's taking place and why.

00001.Jpeg

1.1 The Spiritual Source of Empathy

Empaths will preserve on pain of others too. The motive for this is as an alternative philosophical. Through the Origin (God or the Universe) view, there is no such detail as branch. When we skip down from Source energies via densities or tiers, we preserve to appearance diverse viewpoints and archetypes, before we enter the densest form; our real life.

We have man and lady, person and beast, affection and terror, authentic and lousy, healthy and unhealed, in this scale. When we circulate human form, the critiques are limitless. So our quest is prepared using our room in our coronary coronary heart-the use of love-to transport returned to a country of Oneness. This Oneness is how we are able to understand the Past and how we're able to understand the Future.

Once the ego is raised, they incarnate greater open than most to this promise of Oneness. We normally give you the actual concept of affection-to simply receive honestly each person as your non-public self.

Yet what takes place whilst you don't respect the opportunity? What if the alternative one isn't open to loving and does no longer see the which means of what you do? It causes latent energies to detach existence energy from empathy. It makes working in an surroundings in which we're programmed no longer to percent our genuine truth, enjoy even our inner most feelings, and communicate about our darkest thoughts greater complicated for empathy.

1.2 Why do Empaths Exist?

In short, the purpose why empathies are proper right here is for them to recognize the way to hold their personal energies and constitute every their shadow and mild developments at the same time as preserving the capability to attain into, sense about, recognize, and speak with whomever they encounter. It allows healers revel in empathic inside the direction of themselves and the arena round them. We are presupposed to create unique limits on themselves, irrespective of how they need to bring in high quality human beings's feelings. This self-mastery and the out of doors global are empathy, which recognizes concord with all subjects and with anybody. It's moreover the instinct that is aware about in which they start and finish and at the same time as someone starts offevolved offevolved and finishes in order that they do now not get overwhelmed with resources. If they may be willing to carry out so with themselves, they inspire us to do the identical and cope via organising robust limits, on the identical time as then dealing with their non-public pain, in place of zeroing in on a person else's struggling at the same time as taking it on in reality, throwing oneself at the decrease back burner.

Empathy has a completely particular trajectory and is certainly heightened. This is the transition way, a journey we are all on as nicely, however a ride and approach of which empathy becomes lots greater responsive. Not simplest do they must cope with their non-public loss, however they keep the duty with the collective's loss.

This cycle is complicated due to the reality the greater the traumas of others layer on the guilt, the extra the traumas of the empaths boil again to the floor-being difficult to avoid-

culminating in a complete detox, such that the guilt will restore the preliminary wound in the long run.

Traumas that address emotion generally mimic their private to the identical strength or functionality. This match permits empathy to speak with others and apprehend their non-public wounded as properly. Furthermore, if the character they may be empathizing with is an wrongdoer, such mirroring will purpose a long way more misery. Yet even then, empathy is attempting to strain itself aside and set itself free.

This stopping lower again within the course of the attacker or relentless injustice gives upward push to what's referred to as the Supernova Empath. The Supernova empathy is what empathy is at the same time as it's miles activated via masses tension at the senses, the thoughts, and the spirit, to the point that empathy can unconsciously defend itself through adopting the maximum Narcissistic traits. Not simplest can moreover they have their empathic skills at their fingertips, however they'll however particular each their dormant and acquired manipulative tendencies to apply those attributes toward the sufferer or the deliver in their persecution, the usage of them an prolonged way from often scaring the other for the protection to avoidance of the empathy.

When empathy is unfastened, the Supernova empathy retreats into its state of affairs of being Empathic, and the Narcissistic tendencies sleep over again. Empathy cannot come to be a Narcissist; however, for durability and power safety, empathy should discover ways to reconcile their terrible facets with their high-quality ones.

Pushing lower back closer to violence and injustice becomes a habitual, such that violence and inequality will in the end no longer actually be of the identical degree of empathy.

1.Three Managing Empathy

Empathy has no danger of no longer having empathy. But they may be able to learn how to control their empathy that allows you to no longer weaken them.

To do all of the want for empathy is to come to be consciously aware about their very personal wounds, their own traumas, their own suffering and functionality losses, and compassion for self.

Empaths want to investigate to take care of themselves and number one become aware in their non-public feelings — a idea which can appear virtually overseas however is essential for their motive, survival and properly-being.

Such inclined human beings might also moreover moreover acquire clinical help to keep their physical well-being, try and address subjects themselves, or both. The greater self-conscious Empaths are, the higher they are capable of represent their real selves-and our right self desires to charge and care about itself first.

1.Four Empaths in Relationships

Empaths who have now not managed their ability to be in relationships are usually tough to stay round. If their wounds reflect their companion's wounds or not, love is truely and really in sync with their spouses to such an amazing degree that it is as despite the fact that they'll be jogging as one.

Already, if that grow to be now not controlled, the impact on the partnership may need to grow to be risky.

The explanation is, empathy hasn't managed to installation robust limits for itself and consequently, it cannot obtain this for others but. We additionally experience fear about their partner's "thoughts-studying;" empathies perceive and recognize what's being said through a sixth enjoy, as well as listening and thinking what isn't always being said. This, combined with a companion that has unresolved depression or who is socially faraway in a way that doesn't satisfy the needs of intimacy, will make contributions to co-dependence and a sense of self-loss on each aspects.

The partnership is surely too annoying for the Non-Empath who has unanswered issues to attend to to deal with the power of the interaction. The guilt is hurting from getting have become out from their decide, the pressure of "only looking to help," and the hassle of carrying in their partner's trauma.

When the pair in the end separates, the soreness that loves motives is insurmountable to that of a Non-Empath. Now they need to permit skip of their individual's suffering even as additionally recognizing what drew this accomplice inner them and the unhealed sides interior themselves that pondered their personalities, and getting higher from all of that in addition to getting higher from the divorce.

There is, of direction, a way for Empaths to create and hold stable interactions. When empathies fall into harmony with themselves, partnerships with them are continuously painful, but they emerge as a few issue that parallels Heaven. Empaths grow to be compassionate, sensitive, moist, attuned to problems out of doors the body, sincerely supportive and alluring, but non-judgmental.

This may additionally want to sound as despite the fact that the sensitivity was honestly tailored for the you-a blessing. And that's what they surely are gifted individuals.

1.Five TheEmpath's Journey

In order for empathies to have healthy and rich interactions, they want to cognizance on their friendship with themselves and prevent feeling liable for annoying too profoundly. We need to consider themselves as mild due to the fact as an lousy lot as we are a slight for others, they have to try and recognize being a mild for themselves. Uncovering and coming across some thing it's miles that makes them revel in nugatory and unlovable, confused, mistaken, and the inner pursuit of love is with out a characteristic to name home in the universe-this is the real because of this of the Hero's Journey. They're unfastened until empathies manage to do this.

They are strong-in all their shadow and slight-to love themselves and others without guilt, judgment or terror. We understand that they will be the best they were seeking out in the universe and they cannot simplest offer one but also attempt to accept love from their buddy, and from someone else.

Isn't it what every parents proper right here want to do? Be our very own savior and accept as actual with that we have a propensity to percent our redemption with each one of a kind.

To sum up, having empathy is a nearly tough community that empathy feelings will schooling consultation certainly by way of themselves. Yet it isn't always the case here. Empathies have a tendency to apprehend self-care, self-recognition and self-love. Much of it entails calling out for help. Empaths come here to talk about compassion, concord and the importance of easy obstacles.

We inspire us to transport via their more empathetic side as empathies achieve out to manual, pay interest, and apprehend.

It's not about a psychiatric sickness. It is knowing, energy, and present. The instinct should be able to understand the subjective nature as properly via manual and steering.

1.6 Types of Empathy

Empathy is defined as 'feeling for' others — being capable of characteristic yourself in their function and enjoy positive feelings as even though you had been them. It's pronouncing that empathy is crafted from many separate components.

But there also are severa forms of empathy that psychologists have defined. These embody summary empathy, ethical records and sympathy.

This is an example of what each of those styles of empathy manner. This similarly illustrates how and at the same time as one or greater of the three sorts of empathy can be displayed however behave in a reckless manner.

Cognitive Empathy

Cognitive empathy, moreover referred to as 'thoughts-set-taking,' isn't always quite what any human beings can speak of as empathy. Cognitive empathy will in reality feature your self within the role of someone else to peer that standpoint.

This is a precious capability, for instance, in offers or for managers specially. This lets you vicinity your self within the hands of someone else, with out honestly being entangled of their emotions. But it does no longer genuinely tie in with the idea of empathy as 'feeling with' and is a much greater lower priced and logical operation. Effectively, in preference to emotion, logical empathy is 'empathy via thinking.'

A Dark Side to Cognitive Empathy

This is critical to illustrate emotional understanding without any affiliation or concord for it. It's regular to presume most people will recognize this fellow-feeling as a middle issue of empathy.

Torturers may require strong moral intelligence to determine out the right manner to damage others, albeit without a bargain compassion for them.

Emotional Empathy

Emotional information is whilst you revel in the feelings of the opposite character with them very sincerely, as despite the fact that you would 'caught' the feelings. Often named 'monetary pain' or 'social contagion' is social empathy. It is just like the everyday definition, albeit greater dramatic, of the time period 'empathy.'

Emotional empathy is in all likelihood the primary shape of empathy, every person experience as babies. When a mom smiles at her little one, it may be visible, and the little one 'seize' her emotion and smile again. More fortuitously, perhaps a infant can also frequently start screaming each time he or she sees a few special infant crying.

Emotional Empathy May Be Good or Bad

Emotional know-how is notable, because it guarantees we will with out issues apprehend and enjoy the emotions of various humans. It is essential to encouraging the ones in care careers, collectively with physicians and nurses, to comply efficaciously to their patients. This moreover ensures that whilst they are in hassle, we can also moreover moreover react to colleagues and others.

Emotional empathy is evil when you do not forget that those feelings will overpower you, and because of this can not react. It is diagnosed as empathy fatigue, this is better clarified in our article on Knowing Others. People with a propensity to get the disillusioned need to awareness on self-law, and specially strength of thoughts, so that you can manage their personal emotions higher.

Great strength of mind eases doctors and nurses, now not to over empathize with possible burnout. Nonetheless, there can be a hazard they are able to get 'hardened' and now not react efficiently. Some present day incidents have arisen within the UK, along with in South Staffordshire, wherein nurses and others are suspected of being heartless. It can also were a functionality manufactured from over-safety in competition to overloading of empathy.

Compassionate Empathy

In the end, we typically recognize emotional empathy through empathy: sensing any person's suffering, after which taking steps to assist.

The term compassionate empathy is well matched with which we typically compassionately recognize. Unlike sympathy, compassion is all about sensing all people's ache, but with a more step into an intervention to relieve the hassle.

Compassionate empathy is the handiest form of empathy, commonly. Typically speaking, individuals who choice or require your empathy do not constantly need to do not forget you (cognitive empathy), and honestly do not need to revel in their misery, or worse, to break into tears beside them (i.E., emotional empathy).

Rather, they need you to keep in mind and sympathize with what they'll be passing thru and, critically, both take steps to restore the trouble, that is, actual empathy, or permit them to perform that.

Finding the Balance

Often, cognitive sensitivity can be known as below-emotional. This manner questioning inadequately, and probably perhaps too much rational have a observe. Those in misery can view this as an unsympathetic reaction.

By assessment, cognitive intelligence is exceptional-emotional. So masses perception or feeling can be powerless. Emotions are primeval. Feeling immoderate emotions, especially anxiety brings one again to infancy. Through nature, greater or an awful lot tons less, this makes one a first rate deal less likely to deal with the condition, and definitely plenty a good deal much less probably to take into account and upload justification to it. Helping someone else is genuinely complicated because of the truth you are crushed via your personal feelings. We need to strike the satisfactory aggregate of rationality and sentiment at the same time as working towards emotional empathy. We can also enjoy the struggling of another human, as though it were happening to us, and thereby show an appropriate amount of compassion. We need to in spite of the truth that remain in charge of our very very own feelings on the same time, and upload justification to the case. This ensures we can make smarter options and deliver them enough assist in which and whilst it's miles required.

1.7 Other styles of Empathy

There are special varieties of empathy, which may be as follows:

Somatic Empathy

It's described as physically feeling each person else's pain. When you witness any person suffering, for instance, you may enjoy physical pain too. Anecdotally, once in a while equal twins document facts while the possibility come to be harm, which can be the example of somatic empathy. Of, e.G., if someone gets caught inside the stomach with a ball in a football workout, you could see an echo of somatic emotion, so one or of the fans must double as despite the fact that they have been struck too.

Spiritual Empathy

This is defined as an instantaneous relation to a better being or popularity. It is positioned throughout the Western metaphysical philosophy, and is similar to 'enlightenment,' and decided possible via contemplation.

1.Eight How Does an Emphatic Person Behave and Act

Empathy is a person that is strongly privy to the feelings of those round them, to the quantity of sensing positive emotions. Empaths view the surroundings in any other case from us; they may be keenly aware about people, their resources of misery and what they bodily require. It isn't exceptional emotions of empaths are harm. As a depend range of reality, inside the approach, moreover they enjoy bodily pain. Quite usually, they may even discover a person's motives or in which they come from. In one of a kind terms, interest has a bent to capture up with all of the human beings round them who've skilled that lifestyles.

Most extremely sensitive humans (HSPs) are empathies as properly but there is probably a difference among empathy and HSP. Finding a strong diploma of empathy is excellent one of the 4 developments that render you an HSP, so beyond feelings, HSPs are privy to specific sorts of stimulation. Many empaths are predicted to be fairly reactive, however not all quite responsive people are robotically empathic.

The signs and symptoms below will assist you discover whether or not or not you are an empath or no longer:

an empath closes her eyes

You generally embody and soak up first rate peoples' feelings into yourself

That is the actual, empathic, number one feature. And if they may be announcing they do not screen it, you are sure to choose it up instinctively, irrespective of what all of us else round you are questioning. Even greater than that: you could in reality experience the feeling as even though it's your non-public, basically "absorbing" it or sponging it up.

Whether precisely, that takes area remains a depend of controversy. Yet we also trust people with immoderate costs of empathy often have very healthful replicate neurons — the a part of the mind that scans certainly one of a kind people's emotional signs and works out what they will expect or revel in. In positive phrases, in case you're an empath, you will possibly be able to choose up on subtle variations in speech, frame language, or voice sound that many pass over — and instinctively hit upon what the individual thinks.

Yet the same functioning replicate neurons suggest you are definitely dwelling with the revel in as even though it have been your personal. That may be an exquisite blessing, but at times it can moreover be disturbing and daunting.

Sometimes, particularly while you're in public, you enjoy surprising, overwhelming emotions

This is not in reality in a unmarried-on-one interaction wherein you experience different humans's emotions. This can manifest each second, even without caution, on the identical time as there are one of a kind people around.

When you're an empath, taking walks into public locations can be daunting, as you could discover your self loaded with an emotion that got here from "nowhere" or, greater particularly, from a person else inside the town.

The atmosphere of a room topics to you loads

Maybe predictably, empaths are substantially touchy to their surroundings's "tone" or mood. We thrive while determined through peace and silence, as we really preserve on sure traits internally. Of the identical cause, areas of nature may be inspiring of empathy, whether or not or not it's miles a non violent greenhouse, a adorable mattress room or museum halls. Likewise, noisy or worrying situations can outcomes drain away empathic resources.

You apprehend in which people are coming from

Some empaths can select out no longer to revel in too many feelings, even though positive empaths will never "sense" them in any respect. Yet even the empaths will intuitively understand what a person is attempting to mention, even though it's tough to supply it out. This is the essential characteristic of empathy even more so than feeling sure humans's feelings. Above all, empathy is truly about expertise and being related to others. So that is what it way to get an expertise of wherein people come from.

People view you as an manual and wait for your advice

For such enjoy, their friend additionally needs empathy for guidance, assist, and idea. It helps empaths to be great listeners as nicely, and will frequently wait patiently for someone to mention what they want to say after which respond from the coronary coronary coronary heart.

If that sounds together with you, you in reality understand it could regularly be disturbing too humans don't in reality apprehend how an entire lot of the power it desires so you may be a speaker to the client, so other people take it as a right.

Tragic or violent occasions can certainly spoil you

When you are an empathist, it does no longer matter if a horrible difficulty could no longer show as an awful lot as you, you're already experiencing it to your whole being. You might also seem to "live via" the pain or unhappiness of the incident your self, even in case you're loads of miles away or probable, even though it's a fictitious incidence in a film. This reaction can also be entirely overwhelming.

Empaths, collectively with HSPs, may not do nicely to witness against the law or human catastrophe, specially although it's a movie that many don't forget charming.

You cannot cover your love of pets, animals, or toddlers

Of path, each person is acquainted with babies are sweet little affords, and dogs and cats are lovable however the feelings are a long way greater for you. You will now not be capable of forestall your self with the useful resource of gushing approximately the lovable infant of another, or by using way of crouching down instinctively to provide a puppy a few affection. Many humans can think your response "over the top," but how does a person now not reply this way within the path of you?

It is, in lots of respects, one of the most essential blessings of being an empath. Every now and then, the feelings are switched up immoderate, even specific ones.

You are more likely to feel people's bodily illnesses too, and not honestly their emotional ache

You may also flow into to date as to sense their disorder even as someone is sick or wounded, as even though it were yours. It does no longer most effective include expressing regret or empathy for them however experiencing real bodily emotions inside the identical factors of the body, which includes pain, tightness or soreness. It's as although the empathic brain is not surely mirroring what the alternative individual wants to sense however additionally translating the feeling onto your non-public body physical.

So that can be distracting once in a while crippling. Perhaps it is not a "gift" that maximum empaths want to get. Yet it is also on the coronary heart that empathy is such wonderful carers. We might not be capable of in fact talk with a person who is in misery with out that functionality, or offer them precisely what they need to feel greater comfortable.

Not , the concern is interested by professions such as a nurse, educator, elderly care worker or healer. When you can feel the discomfort after this, it might be adorable at the same time as you didn't determine to do something about it.

You can turn out to be beaten in very close to relationships

Relationships can be hard for every body. Yet assume how an awful lot more such problems are because you could pay attention your accomplice's single little mindset, frustration or, effective, even lie. Yet positive feelings might also moreover turn out to be overwhelming as if you are "engulfed" through the connection.

Yet there's greater to it than that. The social environment is often a mission, as you determine collectively. For empathy, the "coronary coronary heart" of a cohabiting companion is still there, which may also regularly seem like an intruder. Empaths see their homes as a safe haven wherein they're capable of dispose of their emotional senses from the relentless call for and companion shifts that.

Although for this purpose, a few empathies prefer to live on my own, others learn how to adapt — in all likelihood with the useful resource of manner of having a room it sincerely is their personal vicinity, or (extraordinarily vital) with the aid of manner of finding a accomplice who's aware their limitations.

You are talented with the functionality to come across liars

Yes, there have been really moments that someone succeeded in deceiving you ... But even then, you discovered out from the outset that you have been transferring closer to your gut instinct. The problem approximately the willingness of an empath to interpret quality the tiniest social signs way that keeping off one's actual reasons is kind of impossible additionally if you do not know exactly what a person in reality desires, you understand in the occasion that they don't always need to be honest or within the event that they appear shifty.

You find out it virtually tough to apprehend why any chief wouldn't located their groups first

Managers and community managers are normally insensitive and in reality do not pay heed to the wishes in their body of personnel. When you're an empath, it's miles not every disrespectful or annoying it's a management flaw.

It is partially due to the truth empathies themselves will create awesome members, so on the same time as they're able to, it's miles regularly via concerning their colleagues so uniting human beings thru commonplace pastimes. Empaths try and be compassionate and responsive, so any a part of the group is concept. The very last effects is not great a satisfied network of men, and it is the usage of all of the information and making knowledgeable alternatives.

You have this soothing and calming effect on humans spherical you

You have the functionality to assist others better. That is real. Much even as human beings strive empaths for guidance, within the presence of instinct, they frequently enjoy greater comfy. Nevertheless, through tough periods people once in a while unconsciously are searching out out their maximum empathetic associates.

That is what you could genuinely domesticate and use to empower others, within the context of encouraging them to transport through severe emotional trauma to go beyond dysfunctional conduct. Even if you disguise your intelligence and empathy, you cannot do it in case you really want to make a exchange, you want to acquire your records.

You can not see someone in discomfort and will no longer depart with out lending a assisting hand

You cannot stroll beyond someone in want without wondering how you can help them? Are you suffering to expose off your issue for others because of the truth "there may be a mission to do"? Unless the quit result is not any — not even whilst you're worn-out, now not even whilst you are burdened — so you're probably to be empathic.

Perhaps that is why empathy is this type of vital problem of the human race's cute kaleidoscope. Humans are the fantastic devices on their show show with a experience of knowledge, so it's miles difficult not to look — so react to — the desires of others. That's just wherein the restoration electricity of an emotion stems from, and it is some aspect that we want to need further in our manner of life.

You are exceptionally touchy and emotional

Empathy can be very transparent, brief to just accept as authentic with, and very touchy to emotional feelings (whether or not or no longer its private or a person else's).

Such resilience ensures you may reach the best highs, but it nonetheless burdens you with the bottom lows and a tendency to be affected deeply thru broken ties. When you are an empath, each day, you will go through a giant spectrum of feelings, each due to your private reactions to lifestyles and due to what you acquire.

Empaths are generally naïve and as a give up end result turn out to be smooth objectives of manipulators

Your instinct additionally guarantees humans will take gain of you. As a final results, they may pressure you proper into a function in which you satisfy their emotional desires and get treasured little out of your private partnership.

You can also have decided, for example, that you moreover draw narcissists (who are at the alternative give up of the empathy spectrum) and perpetrators (who've to be "rescued" through manner of using stressful human beings). Empaths also need to be careful of who they're permitting into their hands. Empaths are very innovative

The heightened empathic impulses and perceptions supply them an considerable quantity of content material to talk in imaginitive techniques. Whether you are an empath, you're almost continually stimulated via what you are thinking about.

Many empathies are conventional singers, performers, or authors, at the equal time as others are often actors, dancers, or visually expressive. Creative moves, in plenty of conditions, enable empathies to unleash pent-up anger in a extremely good, constructive way.

Empaths are first-rate listeners

Unsurprisingly friends and empathic own family additionally factor out turning into top notch listeners. That is due to the fact becoming a very effective listener lets In you to place your self inside the arms

of the opportunity person; no person is more potent than surely all and sundry intuitively choosing up feelings.

Empathy is constantly real almost about translating the thoughts of a loved one into sentences, supporting them enjoy heard, desired and less by myself. Empathy moreover gravitates into occupations requiring conversation (e.G., counseling and training).

Empaths can not and will now not say no to all of us

https://cd5vo46ju4834fu142zvmudg-wpengine.Netdna-ssl.Com/wp-content/uploads/TheLawOfAttraction_0001_l oa.JpgEmpaths do no longer like to show down the request of a needy character, as they might pay interest the frustration, anger and sorrow in others. It moreover implies they've got so many duties on the street! It is normally this, lamentably, in order to fulfill the needs in their households, own family people or colleagues.

If you're an empath, you're probable too aware about appearing positive human beings's relational interest that you may honestly glaringly extend it to inspire preferred favors, specially despite the fact which you are in spite of the fact that overburdened.

Empaths love nature and herbal splendor

Everyday existence appears to be concerned and chaotic, and empathy prospers in movement isn't any marvel. If you have got got a excessive level of empathy, being out can experience wonderfully quiet and replenishing in massive-open areas. In truth, as required materials in their self-care sporting events, many empaths point out being via the sea or going for walks in the vicinity. Time in nature can come up with a experience of liberation, similarly to supplying peace and quiet.

They are daydreamers

Some of the least essential indicators of empathy are chronic having a pipe dream. Sometimes this is blended with empathy's bright imagination. This then lets you contemplate an infinite variety of situations (in particular highly emotionally evocative situations).

Moreover, daydreaming might also sound like a launch from every day lifestyles. Then, regularly empathies shift to the impact in their inventive minds. This will help relieve you from specific human beings's conflicting feelings surrounding them.

Empaths have the tendency of neglecting themselves

Empaths can also emerge as so centered on fine humans's goals and feelings that they may surely start "tuning" their personal dreams. It will, in hard conditions, make contributions to self-forget about approximately, contributing to bodily or intellectual unwellness. Anyone with excessive rates of empathy has to make investments time consciously observing their very personal emotions and feelings to steer an entire, healthy lifestyles. Regular workout of mindfulness or meditation might also moreover beneficial resource with this, developing a sample of self-mirrored image.

1.9 Reasons Why Empaths Often Feel Lonely

Many citizens are embroiled in compassion and empathy. Sympathy is whilst one feels sorry about each other on the equal time as they'll be in some condition. Empathy is whether or not or now not someone definitely thinks or is aware of what a few other character is feeling from past their reference frame. Empathy's hallmark is the capacity to understand what every distinctive human thinks irrespective of their excessive emotional reputation. We type the universe via intuitions of their very very very own. These extraordinarily reactive individuals are having a difficult time and are experiencing many problems, and one in every of them is a experience of isolation. Below are 9 motives why they're the loneliest of the bunch.

Empaths are notably sensitive

We are the people who normally help to sob on for others. They have a hard time extracting the identical empathy from other guys, who sincerely might not keep close how they experience, due to the truth they may not be as empathetic as they may be. And given how fragile they may be, it's far frequently common for empathies to get injured. We also are asked to red meat up up and in reality purpose them to experience like we lack what it takes while having an emotion is a special electricity.

They cannot distinguish their pain from others

They have a hard time looking to separate the struggling they revel in for others from their very very very own because of the truth they care intensely for them as properly. They're having trouble dealing with the sorrow they have for someone. Sometimes it will become too tough to go through due to the reality the pain that they enjoy is not in their palms.

They are introverts

We want their personal vicinity, and locate it hard to interact with others precisely because we enjoy like they can't keep close them or the love they've got within the route of others. We believe a person is probably able to examine them, this is why they pick out to hold to themselves, to avoid the trouble of having to explain what they are going via.

They are appreciably intuitive

Empathy is alternatively intuitive and frequently is going with the gut. Some won't make experience, however a sense of subject inside the coronary coronary heart isn't always regularly incorrect. It is one of the reasons they do not forget it's miles difficult to get so connected to a person because they apprehend how the partnership could play out. You may as an alternative learn how to deal with the conflicting feelings that they despite the fact that have, as a substitute of having to carry all of us ordinary in.

They are with out problems crushed

We aren't legal to hold too many on the identical time. Around the equal 2d, no individual is probably willing to control a number of feelings, so that is the essential task that most empathies face. We on occasion catch themselves in positions that they've no concept a way to control or keep away from the intellectual surge till it gets to their hearts.

They block their sensitivity, as a result being unapproachable

Empaths are stated to be overly sensitive; for this reason, they will be predisposed to shut out humans. It is because of the fact they receive as genuine with like their conduct is what most humans cannot relate to, and they absolutely take those moves out of worry of being branded normal or perhaps crazy. They worry that it's far going to be difficult for humans to conform.

They permit their beyond rule their emotions

Empaths typically have little fond young people recollections as only some have to have the actual steerage and environment that nurtures their touchy aspect. The abilities that they superior, as a required survival beneficial useful resource as kids, turn out to be becoming a part of their maturity. Perhaps such coping strategies are a good deal less a achievement for an person than they should be for an little one. The pattern with which emotion will cope with the difficulty or ache is the same at the same time as the situation is new.

1.10 The issues handiest Empaths will apprehend

Empaths have the awesome potential to come across and technique exceptional humans's feelings and that could pose a few specific obstacles.

Being mainly reactive to different human beings's feelings makes empathies loving, supportive, and facts. Friends and household seem to look on them for a compassionate ear first, then a weeping hand. Although a good deal of the planet is not capable of location oneself inside the footwear of others, empathy holds a real superpower the willingness to understand someone's factor of view truly when they without a doubt feel their very non-public feelings. Most specially responsive human beings (HSPs) call themselves empathies.

On the opposite detail, precise issues emerge that include being too empathetic. Empaths now and again experience blamed approximately how profoundly they care. They can frequently short get harassed after they juggle all of the emotions that they enjoy from themselves and from others.

There are sure stressful conditions which only a few empathies can honestly understand. One account of some of the ones issues is given below:

Others' feelings can spark off your feelings brief

You had an first rate day. Maybe you obtain some accurate feedback at art work, checked all the gadgets on your to-do list, or you have got got been just feeling particular approximately lifestyles in popular. A partner both is going home, otherwise you visit a friend who is had a lousy day.

You abruptly experience the emotions changing. Your brilliant vibes are lengthy long past, and just like your pal or cherished one; you enjoy depressed or annoyed. This sounds as even though something happens to you on your day. It will make it more difficult for the alternative character to maintain place, as you already should manipulate the identical emotions. It's hard, as an instinct, to split the emotions of a person from your very own.

Compassion can be a burden for the empaths

Empaths are aware about being suggested (or guided to feeling like) that they don't forget "too much" or that they may be "too sentimental," so it is surprising to us that humans do not care more.

Around the same second, being unwilling to show off love for others round you could experience overwhelming and depart you bearing masses of duties you won't be in rate of. Unless you are the only who sees extra pain than the ones round you, it is impossible not to enjoy chargeable for remedying it.

Solitary desires

Non-empathic people can not require an excessive amount of time alone, and a few even though excel constantly with others. If you're an empathic individual who lives with a accomplice or roommates — when you have extroverted friends — you will require extended talks to purpose them to apprehend your lonely dreams.

You want time to embody and take in changes

Empaths can also have problem shifting from excessive-stimulus situations to low-stimulus activities, so vise the other way round. That's why in the path of a noisy collecting, a few can experience a peculiar "hollowness" that could are in reality intimidated rushing into a packed case. We require time to address the lovable trade and all the accompanying feelings.

You struggle with tension or melancholy

While no longer legitimate in any man or woman, handling their mental nicely being is not unusual for them. They is probably suffering with masses of self-doubt, fatigue, and lack of self warranty because they're so susceptible to emotions — together with their emotions. Receiving anger or disappointment from specific people can feel like a ton of bricks hitting you. Empaths will feel the whole style of emotional and bodily outcomes that surround the emotions of others — which encompass insomnia, coronary heart issues, persistent exhaustion and extra. It implies empathies can be compelled to juggle the emotional consequences of each their personal issues and those of others.

Furthermore, all of the empathies have lived their existence feeling remoted from the ones round them, which can also make contributions to alienation. That's why empathies need to take time for them and make their health a concern.

You realize someone is feeling disturbed at the same time as no character else notices

Empaths can revel in on the equal time as a human gets indignant, once in a while instances in advance than they warn us about it. It may be a notable superb as it lets you bear in mind whether or not others are in misery. But it could furthermore locate it not viable to revel in yourself.

Often you overlook approximately to go away emotional area for your self

You realize so strongly for others round you, and your instinct makes you an excellent listener, a therapist and a solver for issues. Yet from time to time, at the same time as you hold in mind yourself, you provide up all of your electricity to others. It is in which prioritizing the inner manner and self-care is so essential. Empathy has to assist itself so it may have the capability to advantage others.

You do not typically recognise which feelings are emanating from your self

Perhaps that is the fantastic persevering with impediment that empathies stumble upon. When you're continuously ingesting unique human beings's emotional facts, it is able to be difficult to recognise what you experience for others rather than your very personal feelings and emotions. It will purpose uncomfortable options, and your "emotions" often take you down the incorrect avenue.

1.Eleven Scientific Theories Behind Empathy

Now which you have a higher sense of whether or now not or not you qualify as empathy, you can surprise what this capability debts for on the planet. Sometimes intuiting others' emotions and thoughts can revel in straightforwardly weird and disheartening. Meanwhile, if you do now not classify as empathy and do not forget yourself being a skeptic of empathy, you're but asking whether or not there in reality is any convincing evidence that those human beings really get up.

When it factors out, there are as a minimum six logical theoretical motives in the back of what might also moreover seem to be a non-conceivable weapon in the beginning appearance. We in short deliver an cause of the findings of the most latest empathy research. Furthermore, we might are searching out to make clear the results it can deliver within the future and assemble a deeper revel in of empathy. This is certainly a thriller that exactly remarkable humans personal an multiplied functionality for empathy; it is mainly probable that one or extra of the above theories may be right.

Sensory Processing Disorder

Sensory processing ailment is a sickness that makes the brain warfare of the affected individual to characteristic via the statistics absorbed from the surroundings round them. This will render you over-touchy to everything from tastes and noises to brushes of slight in your pores and skin. We also can enjoy this cycle as painful. So, even as life is actually too loud or over-stimulating in another way, you could wobble on your feet, force slowly, so locate distance judgment hard. Many may additionally additionally do experience dizziness and heightened anxiety.

So how does empathy make a contribution to any of this? Some scientists moreover indicated that sensory impairment in nice people can also exist on the emotional level. This want to reason them to masses greater aware of other people's emotions. Enhanced empathy, on this opinion, is the intellectual counterpart to experiencing ache at the gentlest touch on the face.

Next, the statistics remains contradictory as to what triggers sensory impairment illness. Several research advise a hereditary component (thus empathies have to have as a minimum one strongly empathic discern), and others relate sensory processing sickness to atypical mind function that takes vicinity in reaction to noise or illumination.

https://cd5vo46ju4834fu142zvmudg-wpengine.Netdna-ssl.Com/wp-content/uploads/empath-traits-1.Jpg

1.12 Empaths Could Have Overactive Mirror Neurons

Mirror neurons are mind cells that have a longtime hyperlink to human emotion inside the simplistic experience. Because of these nerves, for instance, maximum humans will show as a minimum slight empathy, feeling awful on the identical time as a person is suffering, or expressing delight within the midst of the satisfied accomplishment of each different individual. Research indicates that the reflect neurons reply among physicians and sufferers for the duration of empathetic interplay. Brain tests show that those mirror neurons pulse in regions of the mind that lead to sure emotions seen while we see others feeling an emotion. Scientists additionally decided that mirror neurons often play a function in certain animal behavior, particularly primates.

The relation among mirror neurons and empathies is that there is a superb threat that greater neurons will make contributions to more empathy. So if you're an empathist, those thoughts cells also can have a higher than ordinary proliferation. Again a genetic detail is probably to be an area proper right here. Yet work is underway on one-of-a-kind influencing variables. Meanwhile, human beings with a shape of delinquent situation of behavior, for instance, sociopaths and psychopaths, might also moreover have fewer than ordinary mirror neurons.

Electromagnetism

At a barely contrary mindset, Electromagnetism may also additionally moreover clarify all of the above-cited results of empathy. This unique hypothesis stems from severa interesting theorists 'check, who have investigated how our electromagnetic fields are capable of manipulating others' magnetic fields. The effects in particular advocate that our hearts and brains are growing their very own special electromagnetic fields. Such regions are believed as a manner to speak some information concerning the thoughts, options and values of the individual, consisting of the ones folks who aren't natural-born empathies. Such findings of electromagnetism mean empaths may additionally have extra suitable responsiveness of the hearts and brains of those of their proximity to the electromagnetic fields. The moral experience may additionally then come to be so fragile that this cycle will become mentally and bodily onerous. Whether empathies also can do sufficient to control their vulnerability stays an unanswered problem.

Many interesting regions of functionality take a look at embody how the effect on empathy differs primarily based totally absolutely on the statistics the opportunity character presents approximately the environment. If so, we would stop that this suggests some component full-size approximately the capability depth of dating that might boom the various empathy and the alternative individual.

Hormone and Chemical Sensitivities

Sections in empathic behavior additionally can be connected to hormone charges, and neurotransmitter charges (i.E., chemical messengers in our brains).

https://cd5vo46ju4834fu142zvmudg-wpengine.Netdna-ssl.Com/wp-content/uploads/empath-traits-2.Jpg

Dopamine, a neurotransmitter, performs a important function in how we react to gratification (and the way we preserve to assemble behaviors that inspire enjoyment over the long run), is a relatively thrilling candidate. Research of dopamine expenses within the sizeable network indicates that introverts are greater liable to dopamine in place of extroverts. This method introverted individuals maintain to require decrease costs of dopamine to obtain pleasure and entertainment. This propensity is probably generalizing. And, if you're an introverted sensitivity, you could furthermore be greater aware of minor chemical shifts within the frame, like the ones because of different human beings's contact. However, almost about empathy, there can be specific emotions and neurotransmitters in movement.

More research can expose precise links amongst empathy and responsiveness to biology. That, in impact, might also need to contribute to analyze on how we may additionally want to enhance empathy for others who lack it.

Emotions May Be Contagious

They are starting to comprehend exactly how contagious feelings may be. Emotional contagion is likewise a acknowledged phenomenon; it lets in make clean how and while the emotions of those round us are picked up. And the ethical contagion affects the ordinary character. Infants, for starters, scream due to the reality they'll feel wonderful toddlers being irritated. Besides, if one character indicates signs and symptoms and signs and symptoms of anxiety, then it will without trouble start spreading thru a miles broader populace. Good mind also can be infectious. Random acts of kindness figures, for example, imply that humans are greater generous when they experience love, and the effects of acts of kindness additionally practice to others who simply witness love, too.

Remember that empathies can be bodily or mentally more willing to "pick out" emotional contagions and song the results which have for our empirical perception of empathy. The precise method through manner of which this might take area, but, remains uncertain. There's even an excellent bit of empathic thinking proper right right here. Furthermore, emotional contagion work demonstrates how empathy will accomplice itself with excessive excellent, notable and motivating human beings to deliberately capture properly emotions from others.

Synesthesia

The final idea worth exploring is that empathies can undergo a special synesthesia kind. Synesthesia is a neural situation that hyperlinks separate senses that could now not generally be associated. Of starters, whilst you see those colorings, super men and women with synesthesia can experience unique tastes. Some would possibly equate a musical sound with numbers. Furthermore, positive sorts of synesthesia can include sensing scents on the identical time as taking note of music or concerning sure colorations to one in every of a type stimuli inside the frame. Most people claim that it's far a critical element in their creativity; like most humans, they virtually do not understand what existence is like. For the case of empaths, despite the fact that, several scholars have theorized that a few aspect is taking location, termed mirror-contact synesthesia. This form of scenario will essentially require empathy to apprehend what others are questioning. This is described as if such feelings are living in and now not past their private our our bodies. Throughout this opinion, immoderate empathy, like each forms of synesthesia, is a medically benign neurological abnormality that incorporates advantages and annoying situations. In order to in addition discover this idea, scientists might also moreover like to test that empathies frequently seem to have positive, similar kinds of ordinary enjoy synesthesia.

Bottom Line

While there are several extremely good and complicated problems, we've got mounted how empathic

interactions can be described from a logical angle. We have frequently looked at how to differentiate amongst advanced empathy and natural attention. Try to take into account some of the techniques you could get the amazing out of being empathetic. But make certain you maintain protecting your self from some of the related dangers.

CHAPTER 7: Knowing about Introverts, Empaths, and Highly Sensitive People

People normally wander about the distinction among empaths and fairly touchy people. They have versions, but they nevertheless have common tendencies in the identical duration. Empaths preserve all of the "Highly Sensitive Persons" developments or HSPs. Those incorporate a small pain tolerance, the choice for time on my own, susceptibility to noise, sound and fragrance, and an aversion to huge crowds. This often takes longer for especially reactive humans to relax during a entire day, due to the truth the potential of their body to move from immoderate intensity to quietness is gradual. Generally, extremely reactive humans are introverts, and sensitivity can be introverts or extroverts (no matter the reality that maximum are introverts). Empaths particular the splendor of nature, peaceful locations, the capability to manual others and a colorful inner existence of a very responsive person.

Empaths, despite the fact that, are transferring the intensely reactive person's attitude even similarly. In Eastern restoration practices, we are capable of feel an invisible strain, this is called shakti or prana, and in the long run draw it into our non-public bodies from other humans and numerous situations. That's now not generally finished for particularly emotional human beings. This strength lets in one to recognize the forces surrounding us in profoundly insightful techniques. Because all consists of sensitive power like mind and bodily stimuli, we internalize others' discomfort and suffering energetically. Sometimes we have have been given issue isolating the ache of a person from our very very very own. Many empaths additionally have profound non secular and emotional insights that normally are not correlated with pretty sensitive human beings. Others may also additionally have interaction with flora and fauna, with nature, and with their publications internal. Both an incredibly reactive character and having instinct are not strictly precise: at the identical moment, you may be each. Also, many quite sensitive humans are empaths. If you reflect onconsideration on this difference in terms of an empathic continuum, empathy is at the top give up; rather reactive humans are a hint decrease on the size, humans with proper empathy are within the middle of the continuum, but they'll be now not HSPs or empathies. On the lowest cease of the continuum are narcissists, sociopaths and psychopaths who've "empath impaired situations."

https://drjudithorloff.Com/main/wp-content/uploads/2020/06/Difference-between-HSps-and-Empaths2.Jpg

The affords of cognizance and empathy, in particular at this 2d in human improvement, are valuable. We need to preserve increasing our hearts and pushing via the empathetic continuum to new heights.

2.1 Signs of a Highly Sensitive Person

A mainly touchy character (HSP) has a restrained view of the environment than most. Highly touchy people are greater conscious of the subtleties and filter out facts profoundly because of a neurological disparity they may be born with. This method that they live resourceful, sensible, and empathic, however it additionally means that they're more prone to depression and fatigue than most.

While being pretty sensitive is honestly herbal — implying, it is not an infection or scenario — it is once in a while incorrect, due to the truth that high-quality 15 - 20 percentage of the total population are HSPs.

Were you a clever person? When you're associated with any of these symptoms, there is a honest chance you will be an HSP.

You actually dislike cruelty and violence of any kind

A highly sensitive person

All condemn abuse and brutality, but it is able to be very stressful for extremely prone humans to see or observe it. When you can not watch absolutely horrifying, gory, or aggressive films with out being agitated or even becoming bodily unwell, you'll be an HSP. Likewise, you can not be able to deal with a tv record about animal brutality or such violent actions. You're more often emotionally worn-out from information splendid people's emotions and pains.

While alternatively touchy human beings are not inherently empathic, HSPs appear to "take in" the feelings of different humans, just as with an empath. It's commonplace for an HSP to step into location and enjoy the human beings's moods in it right away. That's because of the fact pretty sensitive human beings are very privy to the subtleties that many can pass over — including facial gestures, tone of voice and body language. Pair that with the inherently stepped forward costs of the sensitivity of the affected person, and it is no marvel HSPs experience feelings that don't belong to them. Highly touchy humans preserve to harm from recurrent highbrow fatigue therefore.

Time pressure is terrible for you

In training, you have got been rendered quite nerve-racking via scheduled tempo or quizzes assessments even to the extent of no longer being capable of feature in addition to you typically would. Being an person, you get substantially beaten due to the fact you have got such masses of gadgets for your to-do list, simply now not sufficient time to complete them. HSPs are more privy to stimuli, which isn't any exemption below time call for.

You withdraw frequently

Whether you are an introvert or an extrovert, you require masses, ideally by myself, of downtimes. Often, at the end of a extended day, you find out yourself withdrawing right into a quiet, darkened room relax your senses and refresh to beautify the strain intensity.

You get scared without troubles

You run like a traumatic animal as everybody is looking at you. Most HSPs have a robust "startle response," so their apprehensive systems are known as once more even in non-threatening conditions.

You ponder deeply

The hallmark of being an HSP is that you nicely examine expertise. It shows that you're doing lots of speaking about your reports more than most human beings do. Sadly, that still implies that you are more willing to over-expect negatively. Often you recreate things in your head or glide obsessively through repetitive feelings again and again yet again.

You're always at the appearance-out for solutions to questions

HSPs look for solutions to existence's number one troubles. They are thinking why it's miles the manner things are, and what their function is in all of it. When you are a completely intuitive soul, you can have continuously idea why many humans are not as enthralled as you're with the useful resource of the wonders of human lifestyles and the cosmos.

Sudden and loud noises shock you

A noisy bicycle that roars beyond your house, for instance, can clearly shake you.

Your clothing topics lots to you

You've commonly been sensitive about what you are sporting. You're specially annoyed via using scratchy denim or uncomfortable clothing which encompass trousers with a slim waistband. Obviously, non-HSPs can hate such gadgets too, however an HSP need to pick out their clothing wisely to save you them absolutely. So, if an HSP through chance tires out all of these gadgets, the ache may additionally distract from any of their information.

Your pain-bearing capability is an awful lot much less

Most HSPs are extra susceptible to all sorts of ache —body aches, headaches, burn, and lots of others.—in evaluation to non-HSPs.

Your internal self is lively and present

Again, you have got got a stunning internal universe because of your excessive thinking. You may additionally furthermore have had a few imaginary pals as a infant, cherished delusion-primarily based definitely video games, and have been willing to fantasize. Being an man or woman, you may have fantasies which can be superbly actual.

Change is very scary for you

HSPs, draw secure haven from their conduct for the motive that vintage is a first rate deal an awful lot much less exciting than the completely new stuff. This is why transition — each right and dangerous — may even throw away HSPs. For starters, HSPs may be as depressed as they will be extremely happy when they date a person new or having a bit vending. HSPs normally require more timc to comply to transition than others.

At times, your surrounding is your enemy

Similarly, it can be pretty daunting with the intention to glide to a brand new home or fly (however the reality that it is simplest a "right" excursion!) for the cause that senses are flooded with such some of precise tales.

You're extra than frequently misunderstood

Even strong sensitivity is mislabeled. You may be labeled "disturbing" or "shy," and the inference can also have been that there can be some aspect wrong with you. Likewise, exceptional HSPs are categorised as introverts, as advantageous functions overlap HSPs and introverts, which includes having masses of downtimes. In truth, 30 percentage of HSPs are extroverts, even though.

You get hungry and indignant without troubles

HSPs seem like vulnerable to will increase in blood sugar portions, and in the occasion that they have now not eaten in a while, they will get very "hangry" (hungry + irritated).

Highly sensitive humans and stimulants

Many HSPs are aware of caffeine and require a completely small amount of it to experience their buzz. Likewise, positive HSPs are sensitive to the outcomes of alcohol, too.

Conflict is venom for you

If your near partnerships incorporate friction or warfare, you sense it intensely. Some HSPs moreover record having a physical infection at some point of the dispute. As a final consequences, some fantastically touchy human beings do or say almost the whole thing to make the opportunity individual glad. That is because of the fact there is a lot harm from battle of phrases.

Criticism is a dagger for you

HSPs virtually expect for Terms. The right language will deliver them to fly; but, blunt language can crash them to the earth. Criticism may moreover sound like a knife, and complaint is negative to the finely balanced form of the especially reactive character. You're conscientious

You are jogging difficult no longer to make mistakes at artwork and in college. It does not, of path, mean that you are remarkable. De facto, no man or woman is splendid. Yet you are however throwing the overall paintings into stuff.

You're virtually moved through adorable and spell binding topics

Good meals, warmth fragrances, lovely artwork or transferring melodies have a important effect on you. You can also take a look at the song or one-of-a-type noises place you in a near trance-like circumstance, or you might be awestruck via the way the breeze captures the leaves within the autumn sunshine. You do now not understand if you're now not as laid low with beauty as many people are.

You're pretty perceptive

You are referred to as insightful and informed because you discover stuff that many overlooks. You can also were realistic even as a boy, beyond your age. The planet is based upon on humans such as you who're extremely receptive to make it a worrying, tolerant location to stay.

The difference amongst Empaths, Introverts, and Highly Sensitive People

We every so often put together introverts, empathizes and those who are specifically reactive. While they percent extremely good not unusual tendencies, they will be very excellent from each specific. And what's the difference and do you watch yourself falling into one or more corporations of this type? Let's take a look at this one.

Introverts

Lately, there was a lot communicate round introverts, and maximum humans already understand that becoming an introvert could not robotically render you concerned or unsociable. Yes, even introverts are friendly folks who need to spend time with a couple of real pals. During such social settings, even though, introverts get exhausted resultseasily and want lots of time by myself to maintain their belongings. That's why introverts every so often enjoy closing domestic or sharing time with handiest one or two human beings in choice to a giant community. Having an introvert is inherited, so it consists of versions in the way in which the mind produces dopamine, the chemical "reward." Individuals raised as introverts in truth don't revel in motivated via social stimulation like gatherings or gossips, and due to this, they get harassed out pretty without problems in such instances. Most introverts, but, derive profound pride from amusing matters which includes studying, creative interests and calm reflected photo.

You're an extended manner more an introvert than an extrovert in case you're a appreciably sensitive person (HSP). Around 70% of HSPs are often stated to be introverts and it makes sense that they are regularly wrong with every exceptional. An particularly reactive introvert may be very observant, compassionate, mild, and willing to apprehend exclusive human beings nicely no matter the truth that others crush them. You can also be an introvert and not specifically reactive. It may also moreover appear like alternatively "in touch" with others due to the fact many individuals are the handiest item on their display with HSPs. This might also additionally suggest less tension from first-rate types of stimuli, at the side of time strain, brutal video sequences, loud sounds, and lots of others. Even if you do require lots of time by myself. In addition:

• Introverts are about 30-50 percent of the residents.

• Many introverts are neither especially reactive nor empathic.

• Introversion is a man or woman trait this is widely diagnosed and is different from the opportunity .

Empaths

Lately, the term "empath" has taken on a unique significance. At a factor, it changed into regularly utilized in technology fiction to become aware of an individual with exquisite talents to understand different humans's emotional and mental situations. Even despite the fact that many humans but equate empaths with a theological element, the time period has come to be more famous in recent times. Today it is usually suggested someone who's surprisingly informed of the feelings of others spherical them. And that is what it looks like. Empaths might probable claim that they do no longer typically "recollect" the thoughts of others; as an alternative, the technique is that of eating their feelings. It's as despite the fact that empaths sense the emotions of someone proper next to them. It can also encompass real signs and symptoms and symptoms. When conquer via overwhelming feelings, she argues that empaths can undergo panic assaults, insomnia, consistent tiredness, and bodily symptoms that contradict conventional medical remedy.

This electricity, for empaths, is every a blessing and a curse. It may be tense due to the truth certain empaths bear in mind they cannot "near it off," so it takes years for them to discover strategies to replace it off as essential. As a outcome, empaths will switch from being truely comfortable to be overcome thru ache, worry, or distinctive emotions merely because of the fact someone else came into the vicinity. Around the same 2d, their largest asset is the willingness of an empath to approach feelings. It helps them to analyze and communicate with others in a sizable manner. It's additionally what receives them exceptional caretakers, buddies, and spouses particularly at the same time as others apprehend their expertise and enjoy it. Like HSPs, empaths have a sturdy intuitive functionality, pretty tuned senses, and can take time to decompress by myself.

• Extroverts or Introverts may be empaths

• "Absorbing" feelings maximum honestly occurs via the use of taking over and internalizing implicit social/emotional signals an involuntary mechanism that empathy can not commonly adjust

• Most of the empaths are probable quite touchy

Highly touchy people

Highly touchy humans are frequently wrong, as are introverts and empaths. It's well-known to apply the term "touchy" as even though it's a bad issue, which additionally implies HSPs get a terrible popularity. Yet the truth is, being fairly aware guarantees you're truely storing extra data about the environment round you than maximum human beings do. This would now not mechanically mean that you're "effects insulted," or that you sob at a hat drop. That guarantees for HSPs:

• Consider problems virtually carefully and find hyperlinks one of a kind human beings do not make

• Often get exhausted or over-stimulated as your mind strategies an excessive amount of feedback (specially in mainly stimulating environments along with a party or engaged study room);

• Using motivational signals, including regret, and show profound assignment in the direction of others

• Note tiny and diffused facts that humans every so often miss (together with patterns and mild noises)

In distinct terms, being fantastically sensitive possesses an emotional element to it, and regularly HSPs will perceive as empathies whats up seem to enjoy distinct humans's feelings a whole lot as empaths do. Around a similar time, turning into an HSP often approach becoming more sensitive to everything, no longer genuinely feelings, sensory stimuli. In situations which are without a doubt too loud, busy, or abruptly paced, HSPs can get frustrated whether or not there are particular feelings to cope with or now not. Low vigilance has been studied properly, as has introversion. Autism is at the complete inherited, which includes masses of subtle mind versions. This is also a herbal, balanced function expressed through up to twenty percent of the populace.

• Extroverts or Introverts or can be HSPs

• The bulk (if now not all) of HSPs are probably clearly empathic

• HSPs and Empaths may be the 2 facets of a not unusual function, as extra empathy is researched

The Connection amongst Empaths, Introverts, and HSPs

Among such characteristics, there can be overlaps, and there's sufficient proof for it. An character can be all three — a pretty touchy, introverted empath — or one or of them can be either. After all, those are person traits, and the temperament of each is specific. Nonetheless, as a desired, most empaths are expected to be exceptionally touchy human beings. Lots of the traits that we assign to empaths are nice traits of Highly Sensitive People underneath any other name. All HSP can "take in" distinct people's emotions, however the ones who do are without a doubt empaths. The opposites of introverts, empaths and HSPs are being referred to underneath:

The contrary of an introvert

The introvert's opposite is an extrovert. Often it's miles claimed that extroverts derive their electricity from social conditions. They have a "contact tank" an extended manner longer than the introverts, and their minds are designed to get severa gratification from the ones situations.

The opposite of immoderate sensitivity or empathy

A narcissist is frequently assumed to be the inverse of empathy or emotional interest, but that is in fact no longer legitimate. Even as being significantly sensitive (or empathetic) is right, being heaps much less so also can be a immoderate best characteristic.

Most touchy people are certainly no longer as inspired through the sensations that accompany them. Even as immoderate sensitivity in some events can be specifically beneficial, it is able to additionally be beneficial to be a whole lot a lot less sensitive particularly in noisy, demanding conditions together with manufacturing the military, worksites, and others. Those individuals aren't inherently grasping or selfish.

00008.Jpeg